JOHN
MACARTHUR

1&2 PETER

~ *Courage in Times of Trouble* ~

THOMAS NELSON
Since 1798

NASHVILLE   DALLAS   MEXICO CITY   RIO DE JANEIRO   BEIJING

1 & 2 PETER
MACARTHUR BIBLE STUDIES

Copyright © 2007, John F. MacArthur, Jr.

Published in Nashville, Tennessee. Thomas Nelson is a trademark of Thomas Nelson, Inc.

Thomas Nelson, Inc. titles may be purchased in bulk for education, business, fundraising, or sales promotional use. For information, please email SpecialMarkets@ThomasNelson.com.

Produced with the assistance of the Livingstone Corporation. Project staff include Jake Barton, Betsy Todt Schmitt, and Andy Culbertson.

Project editors: Mary Horner Collins, Amber Rae, and Len Woods.

Scripture quotations marked NKJV are taken from *The Holy Bible*, New King James Version˙. Copyright © 1979, 1980, 1982, 1992 Thomas Nelson, Inc. Publishers.

"Keys to the Text" material taken from the following sources:

James. MacArthur New Testament Commentary Series. Copyright © 1998 by John MacArthur. Published by Moody Press, Chicago, Illinois. Used by permission.

The MacArthur Study Bible (electronic edition), John MacArthur, General Editor. Copyright © 1997 by Word Publishing. All rights reserved. Used by permission.

Nelson's New Illustrated Bible Dictionary, Rev. ed. R. F. Youngblood, F. F. Bruce, R. K. Harrison, editors. Copyright © 1995 by Thomas Nelson Publishers. Used by permission.

Our Sufficiency in Christ (electronic edition). Copyright © 1991, 1997 by John MacArthur. Published by Word Publishing: Dallas, TX. Used by permission.

Romans. MacArthur New Testament Commentary Series. Copyright © 1994, 1996 by John MacArthur. Published by Moody Press, Chicago, Illinois. Used by permission.

Cover Art by Kirk Luttrell, Livingstone Corporation
Interior Design and Composition by Joel Bartlett, Livingstone Corporation

ISBN-10: 1-4185-0890-X
ISBN-13: 978-141850-890-6

Printed in the United States of America.
07 08 09 10 RRD 9 8 7 6 5 4

CONTENTS

Introduction to 1 Peter

This letter has always been identified with the name of the author, Peter (one of Jesus' disciples), and with the notation that it was his first inspired letter.

Author and Date

The opening verse of the epistle claims it was written by Peter, who was clearly the leader among Christ's apostles. The Gospel writers emphasize this fact by placing his name at the head of each list of apostles (Matt. 10; Mark 3; Luke 6; Acts 1), and including more information about him in the four Gospels than any person other than Christ. Originally known as Simon (Greek) or Simeon (Hebrew)—see Mark 1:16; John 1:40–41—Peter was the son of Jonas, who was also known as John (Matt. 16:17; John 1:42), and a member of a family of fishermen who lived in Bethsaida and later in Capernaum. Andrew, Peter's brother, brought him to Christ (John 1:40–42). Peter was married, and apparently his wife accompanied him in his ministry (Mark 1:29–31; 1 Cor. 9:5).

Peter was called to follow Christ early on in His ministry (Mark 1:16–17), and was later appointed to apostleship (Matt. 10:2; Mark 3:14–16). Christ renamed him *Peter* (Greek), or *Cephas* (Aramaic), both words meaning "stone" or "rock" (John 1:42). The Lord clearly singled out Peter for special lessons throughout the Gospels (for example, Matt. 10; 16:13–21; 17:1–9; 24:1–7; 26:31–33; John 6:6; 21:3–7, 15–17). He was the spokesman for the Twelve, articulating their thoughts and questions as well as his own. Peter's triumphs and weaknesses are chronicled in the Gospels and in Acts 1–12.

After Jesus' resurrection and ascension, Peter initiated the plan for choosing a replacement for Judas (Acts 1:15). After the coming of the Holy Spirit (Acts 2:1–4), he was empowered to become the leading gospel preacher from the Day of Pentecost on (Acts 2–12). Peter also performed notable miracles in the early days of the church (Acts 3–9), and he opened the door of the gospel to the Samaritans (Acts 8) and to the Gentiles (Acts 10). According to tradition, Peter had to watch as his wife was crucified, but he encouraged her with the words, "Remember the Lord." When it came time for him to be crucified, Peter reportedly pled that he was not worthy to be crucified like his Lord, but rather should be crucified upside down (ca. AD 67–68), which tradition says he was.

Because of Peter's unique prominence, the early church had no shortage of documents falsely claiming to be written by him. That the apostle Peter is the author of 1 Peter, however, is certain. The material in this letter bears definite resemblance to his messages in the book of Acts. The letter teaches, for example, that Christ is the Stone rejected by the builders (2:7–8; Acts 4:10–11) and that Christ is no respecter of persons (1:17; Acts 10:34). Peter teaches his readers to be clothed with humility (5:5), reminiscent of the Lord girding Himself with a towel and washing the disciples' feet (John 13:3–5). Other statements in the letter echo Christ's sayings (4:14; 5:7, 8). Moreover, the author claims to have been a witness of Christ's sufferings (5:1; see also 3:18; 4:1). In addition to these internal evidences, it is noteworthy that the early Christians universally recognized this letter as the work of Peter.

The only significant doubt to be raised about Peter's authorship arises from the rather classical style of Greek employed in the letter. Some have argued that Peter, being an "uneducated" fisherman (Acts 4:13), could not have written in sophisticated Greek, especially in light of the less classical style of Greek employed in the writing of 2 Peter. This argument has a good answer, however. In the first place, that Peter was uneducated does not mean that he was illiterate, but only that he was without formal, rabbinical training in the Scriptures. Moreover, though Aramaic may have been Peter's primary language, Greek would have been a widely spoken second language in Palestine. It is also apparent that at least some of the authors of the New Testament, though not highly educated, could read the Greek of the Old Testament Septuagint (see James's use of the Septuagint in Acts 15:14–18).

Beyond these evidences of Peter's ability in Greek, Peter also explained (5:12) that he had written this letter "by Silvanus," also known as Silas. Silvanus was likely the messenger designated to take this letter to its intended readers. But more than that, Peter is acknowledging that Silvanus served as his secretary, or amanuensis. Dictation was common in the ancient Roman world (for example, Paul and Tertius; Rom. 16:22), and secretaries often could aid with syntax and grammar. So, Peter, under the superintendence of the Spirit of God, dictated the letter to Silvanus, while Silvanus, who also was a prophet (Acts 15:32), may have aided in some of the composition of the more classical Greek.

First Peter was most likely written just before or shortly after July, AD 64, when the city of Rome burned, thus having a writing date of about AD 64–65.

BACKGROUND AND SETTING

When the city of Rome burned, the Romans believed that their emperor, Nero, had set the city on fire, probably because of his incredible lust to build. In order to build more, he had to destroy what already existed. The Romans were totally devastated. Their culture, in a sense, had gone down with the city. All the religious elements of their life had been destroyed—their great temples, shrines, and even their household idols had been burned. This had great religious implications because it made them believe that their deities had been unable to deal with this conflagration and also had been victims of it. The people were homeless and helpless. Many had been killed. Their bitter resentment was severe, so Nero realized that he had to redirect the hostility.

The emperor's chosen scapegoat was the Christian community. Christians were already hated because they were associated with Jews and because they were seen as being hostile to the Roman culture. Nero quickly spread the word that the Christians had set the fires. As a result, a vicious persecution against Christians began and soon spread throughout the Roman Empire, touching places north of the Taurus mountains, like Pontus, Galatia, Cappadocia, Asia, and Bithynia (1:1), and impacting the Christians, whom Peter calls "pilgrims." These pilgrims, who were probably Gentiles for the most part (1:14, 18; 2:9–10; 4:3), possibly had been led to Christ by Paul and his associates. But they needed spiritual strengthening because of their sufferings. Thus the apostle Peter, under the inspiration of the Holy Spirit, wrote this epistle to strengthen them.

Peter wrote that he was in "Babylon" when he penned the letter (5:13). Three locations have been suggested for this Babylon. First, a Roman outpost in northern Egypt was named Babylon; but that place was too obscure, and there are no reasons to think that Peter was ever there. Second, ancient Babylon in Mesopotamia is a possibility; but it is quite unlikely that Peter, Mark, and Silvanus had been at this rather small, distant place at the same time. Third, "Babylon" is an alias, perhaps even a code word, for Rome. In times of persecution, writers exercised unusual care not to endanger Christians by identifying them. Peter, according to some traditions, followed James and Paul and died as a martyr near Rome about two years after writing this letter. If this is true, then he had written this epistle near the end of his life, probably while staying in the imperial city. He did not want the letter to be found and the church to be persecuted, so he may have hidden its location under the code word, "Babylon," which aptly fit because of the city's idolatry (Rev. 17–18).

HISTORICAL AND THEOLOGICAL THEMES

Because the believers addressed were suffering escalating persecution (1:6; 2:12, 19–21; 3:9, 13–18; 4:1, 12–16, 19), Peter wrote this letter to teach them how to live victoriously in the midst of that hostility: (1) without losing hope; (2) without becoming bitter; (3) while trusting in their Lord; and (4) while looking for His second coming. Peter wished to impress on his readers that by living an obedient, victorious life under duress, a Christian can actually evangelize his or her hostile world (1:14; 2:1, 12, 15; 3:1–6, 13–17; 4:2; 5:8–9).

Believers are constantly exposed to a world system energized by Satan and his demons whose effort is to discredit the church and to destroy its credulity and integrity. One way these spirits work is by finding Christians whose lives are not consistent with the Word of God and then parading them before the unbelievers to show how the church is a sham. Christians, however, must stand against the enemy and silence the critics by the power of their holy lives.

In this epistle, Peter is rather effusive in reciting two categories of truth. The first category is positive and includes a long list of blessings bestowed on Christians. As he speaks about the identity of Christians and what it means to know Christ, Peter mentions one privilege and blessing after another. Interwoven into this list of privileges is the catalog of suffering. Christians, though most greatly privileged, should also know that the world will treat them unjustly. Their citizenship is in heaven and they are strangers in a hostile, Satan-energized world. The Christian life, therefore, can be summarized as a call to victory and glory through the path of suffering. Thus the basic question that Peter answers in this epistle is: How are Christians to deal with animosity? The answer features practical truths and focuses on Jesus Christ as the model of one who maintained a triumphant attitude in the midst of hostility.

First Peter also answers other important practical questions about Christian living such as: Do Christians need a priesthood to intercede with God for them (2:5–9)? What should be the Christian's attitude to secular government and civil disobedience (2:13–17)? What should a Christian employee's attitude be toward a hostile employer (2:18)? How should a Christian woman conduct herself (3:3–4)? How can a believing wife win her unbelieving husband to Christ (3:1–2)?

Interpretive Challenges

First Peter 3:18–22 stands as one of the most difficult New Testament texts to translate and interpret. For example, does "Spirit" in 3:18 refer to the Holy Spirit or to Christ's Spirit? Did Christ preach through Noah before the Flood, or did He preach in person after the crucifixion (3:19)? Was the audience to this preaching composed of humans in Noah's day or demons in the abyss (3:19)? Does 3:20–21 teach baptismal regeneration (salvation), or salvation by faith alone in Christ? These questions are addressed in the notes.

WHAT AN INHERITANCE!

DRAWING NEAR

As children, we eagerly anticipated holidays or special events. Peter opens his letter with a reminder of what we can look forward to—a glorious future in heaven. Do you eagerly anticipate heaven? Why or why not?

How can looking toward heaven be a comfort in tough times?

As you begin this study of 1 Peter, what do you hope to learn? Ask God to reveal fresh insights and show you how to live them out.

THE CONTEXT

Peter wrote this letter to followers of Jesus Christ scattered across the Roman Empire who were facing increasing persecution. This targeting of believers likely began in the wake of the Emperor Nero's burning of Rome, an act he then promptly blamed on Christians. As the preeminent apostle at the time, Peter recognized the great need to help his maligned and mistreated brothers and sisters gain a right perspective and stand firm in the midst of this suffering. So taking pen in hand, he reminded his audience of the certainty of the future inheritance that is guaranteed to every believer in Jesus Christ. This marvelous future is preserved by the power of God (1:3–5), is proven by the trials of persecution (1:6–9), and was predicted by the prophets of God (1:10–12).

In short, Peter knew it was important for these Jewish believers to look beyond their immediate circumstances to the bedrock truths of the faith. Remembering the eternal promises of the gospel would give them the ability to endure hard times. More than that, living out the down-to-earth, everyday implications of the gospel would present the Christians with numerous opportunities to be positive and hopeful witnesses in a negative and hostile culture. First Peter reveals the warm, caring, pastor's heart of its author. It overflows with hope and is filled with wisdom, making it imminently relevant for our lives today.

KEYS TO THE TEXT

Inheritance: As God's beloved children, we stand to inherit the great riches of salvation—life, righteousness, peace, joy, perfection, God's presence, eternal rewards, etc. The concept of an inheritance from God had great significance to early Jewish believers in Christ because their Old Testament forefathers received the land of Canaan as an inheritance as part of God's covenant with Abraham (Gen. 12:1). Theirs was for the most part an earthly, material inheritance, though it included many spiritual blessings. Our inheritance in Christ, however, is primarily spiritual. That is, it is not a promise of wealth and material prosperity. It goes far beyond cheap temporal or transient physical blessings. We inherit: (1) *God.* David said, "The LORD is the portion of my inheritance" (Ps. 16:5). We are His and He is ours. What a joy to know that we inherit God Himself and will spend eternity in His presence! (2) *Christ.* Believers enter into an eternal oneness with Christ. Christ Himself indwells them (Col. 1:27). (3) *The Holy Spirit.* He is the Guarantor of our inheritance (Eph. 1:14). (4) *Salvation.* This is our full and final deliverance from the power and presence of sin, and from grief, pain, death, and judgment. No matter how difficult our present circumstances might be, we can look beyond them and bless God for the ultimate fullness of our eternal salvation.

UNLEASHING THE TEXT

Read 1:1–12, noting the key words and definitions next to the passage.

1 Peter 1:1–12 (NKJV)

1 Peter, an apostle of Jesus Christ, to the pilgrims of the Dispersion in Pontus, Galatia, Cappadocia, Asia, and Bithynia,

2 elect according to the foreknowledge of God the Father, in sanctification of the Spirit, for obedience and sprinkling of the blood of Jesus Christ: Grace to you and peace be multiplied.

3 Blessed be the God and Father of our Lord Jesus Christ, who according to His abundant mercy has begotten us again to a living hope through the resurrection of Jesus Christ from the dead,

4 to an inheritance incorruptible and undefiled and that does not fade away, reserved in heaven for you,

5 who are kept by the power of God through faith for salvation ready to be revealed in the last time.

6 In this you greatly rejoice, though now for a little while, if need be, you have been grieved by various trials,

7 that the genuineness of your faith, being much more precious than gold that perishes, though it is tested by fire, may be found to praise, honor, and glory at the revelation of Jesus Christ,

8 whom having not seen you love. Though now you do not see Him, yet believing, you rejoice with joy inexpressible and full of glory,

9 receiving the end of your faith—the salvation of your souls.

10 Of this salvation the prophets have inquired and searched carefully, who prophesied of the grace that would come to you,

pilgrims (v. 1)—strangers dispossessed in a land not their own; temporary residents or foreigners

the Dispersion (v. 1)—the sovereign scattering of believers around the world

Pontus . . . Bithynia (v. 1)—the region that makes up modern-day Turkey

elect (v. 2)—from the Greek word that means "called out ones"; the idea here is selection by God for salvation, a comforting concept to those facing persecution

foreknowledge (v. 2)—not just an awareness of future events but a predetermined relationship; God's planning before the fact, not His mere observation before the fact

sprinkling of the blood of Jesus Christ (v. 2)—an allusion to Moses' sprinkling sacrificial blood on the people of Israel as a symbol of sealing their covenant to obey God, as well as a reminder that Christ's blood completely atones for sin and brings the believer into the New Covenant

has begotten us again (v. 3)—a reference to the new birth (see John 3), whereby a believing sinner is born anew into God's family and receives a new nature

hope (v. 3)—not wishful thinking but confident optimism based on the promise and person of God

incorruptible (v. 4)—These heavenly riches are not subject to passing away or undergoing decay.

greatly rejoice (v. 6)—The Christian who truly understands his or her future can experience an exuberant jubilation unrelated to the circumstances of life.

receiving . . . salvation (v. 9) —"Receiving" can literally be translated "presently receiving for yourselves" so that the idea is an immediate deliverance from the power of sin. Ultimate salvation will further deliver us from the presence of sin.

the Spirit of Christ who was in them (v. 11)—Jesus Christ, in the person of the Holy Spirit, took up residence within the writers of Old Testament Scripture, enabling them to reveal the glorious salvation to be consummated in the future.

11 *searching what, or what manner of time, the Spirit of Christ who was in them was indicating when He testified beforehand the sufferings of Christ and the glories that would follow.*

12 *To them it was revealed that, not to themselves, but to us they were ministering the things which now have been reported to you through those who have preached the gospel to you by the Holy Spirit sent from heaven—things which angels desire to look into.*

1) What is significant about calling believers "pilgrims"? What does this term suggest for us as modern-day believers?

_____

_____

_____

_____

_____

2) How does Peter describe the inheritance that awaits believers in Jesus Christ?

_____

_____

_____

_____

3) What insights into "trials" does Peter give his readers in this passage? What purpose do they serve?

_____

_____

_____

_____

(Verses to consider: 2 Cor. 4:16–18; James 1:2–8; Rom. 5:3–5)

4) Peter mentions the fact that his readers have never seen Christ, nor do they see Him in their current trials (vv. 8–9). What is his implied point?

_____

_____

_____

_____

_____

(Verses to consider: Heb. 11:1; John 20:29; 2 Cor. 5:7)

5) What surprising insights are revealed about the Old Testament prophets and angels?

_____

_____

_____

_____

_____

GOING DEEPER

Read the following passage from Ephesians 1:3–14, and see what the apostle Paul reveals about the spiritual inheritance that is promised to all who believe.

3   *Blessed be the God and Father of our Lord Jesus Christ, who has blessed us with every spiritual blessing in the heavenly places in Christ,*

4   *just as He chose us in Him before the foundation of the world, that we should be holy and without blame before Him in love,*

5   *having predestined us to adoption as sons by Jesus Christ to Himself, according to the good pleasure of His will,*

6   *to the praise of the glory of His grace, by which He made us accepted in the Beloved.*

7   *In Him we have redemption through His blood, the forgiveness of sins, according to the riches of His grace*

8   *which He made to abound toward us in all wisdom and prudence,*

9   *having made known to us the mystery of His will, according to His good pleasure which He purposed in Himself,*

9

10 *that in the dispensation of the fullness of the times He might gather*
    together in one all things in Christ, both which are in heaven and which
    are on earth—in Him.

11 *In Him also we have obtained an inheritance, being predestined according*
    to the purpose of Him who works all things according to the counsel of His
    will,

12 *that we who first trusted in Christ should be to the praise of His glory.*

13 *In Him you also trusted, after you heard the word of truth, the gospel of*
    your salvation; in whom also, having believed, you were sealed with the
    Holy Spirit of promise,

14 *who is the guarantee of our inheritance until the redemption of the*
    purchased possession, to the praise of His glory.

Exploring the Meaning

6) What more do you learn about our glorious spiritual inheritance? What
is the Holy Spirit's role in this?

_____

_____

_____

_____

7) Both Peter and Paul explicitly state that God "chooses" people for
salvation. What does this mean? What should be our response?

_____

_____

_____

_____

8) Three times in Ephesians 1:3–14 salvation is said to be "to the praise of
His glory." In 1 Peter 1:7 we find the phrase "praise, honor, and glory." What
do God's praise and glory have to do with salvation?

_____

_____

_____

_____

Truth for Today

Man is redeemed for the purpose of restoring the divine image marred by sin. Because God's intention in creating men was that they should bear the divine image, salvation's goal is creation's goal. God desires creatures that will give Him glory by both proclaiming and displaying His glory. For that reason He redeems men.

Scripture always presents salvation from God's side, in order that He should have full credit. In our humanly oriented society, God's wanting exclusive credit seems inappropriate—but only because men have no concept of His greatness, holiness, and glory. What views they may have of Him are simply projections of themselves. The praise and glory that men so much desire are totally undeserved, and their motives for wanting them are purely sinful. But God seeks glory for the right reason—because He alone is deserving of it. His seeking glory is a holy desire, for He is supremely worthy.

Reflecting on the Text

9) What does your salvation and your eternal inheritance mean to you? What was your life like before?

_____

_____

_____

_____

_____

10) Peter reminded his readers of the fact that the prophets of old "searched carefully" their own writings for hints of the details of the coming of God's great salvation. Why are so many modern-day believers so blasé about their faith and about the incredible inheritance they have in Christ?

_____

_____

_____

_____

_____

11) What are some practical ways this week that you can joyfully live out the truth that you are a pilgrim on this earth?

_____

_____

_____

_____

12) Do you know a fellow believer who is suffering because of his/her faith? How can you offer them encouragement, much as Peter did for his Christian brothers and sisters?

_____

_____

_____

_____

Personal Response

Write out additional reflections, questions you may have, or a prayer.

_____

_____

_____

_____

_____

_____

_____

_____

THE IMPORTANCE OF
AN ETERNAL PERSPECTIVE

DRAWING NEAR

When have you been most gripped by the reality of eternity and the importance of living a holy life? What were the circumstances that prompted this seriousness about spiritual matters?

_____

_____

_____

What do you think is the reason behind the human preoccupation with trivial concerns and living for the here-and-now?

_____

_____

_____

THE CONTEXT

Is it possible for a group of Christians who are facing escalating persecution to live victoriously and joyously in the midst of such hostility? The apostle Peter asserts that not only is it possible; it's necessary! Writing to believers scattered across Asia Minor, Peter urged a lifestyle rooted in hope, void of bitterness, and focused on the second coming of the Lord.

It is, in fact, the certainty of our future inheritance that forms the basis for a victorious Christian experience. As believers become more and more convinced of the sure promises of God, they begin to discover in this life (even in the midst of trials) the marvelous consequences of that future inheritance. Such faith enables them to experience the perseverance of hope (1:13–16), the persistence of wonder (1:17–21), the power of love (1:22–2:3), and the praises of Christ (2:4–10).

As you dig into this meaty epistle, ask God to open your spiritual eyes and ears so that you might more fully appreciate the eternal riches that belong to you as a chosen child of God.

KEYS TO THE TEXT

Holy: From the Greek word *hagios,* holiness means being set apart for a special purpose. In secular and pagan Greek society the word carried no idea of moral or spiritual purity. The manmade gods were as sinful and degraded as the men who made them, and there simply was no need for a word that represented righteousness. Christianity sanctified the term, using it to describe God, godly people, and godly things. Holiness essentially defines the Christian's new nature and conduct in contrast with his pre-salvation lifestyle. The reason for practicing a holy manner of living is that Christians are associated with the holy God and must treat Him and His Word with respect and reverence. We therefore glorify Him best by being like Him.

Redeemed: To buy back someone from bondage by the payment of a price. The imagery behind this Greek word comes from the ancient slave market. It meant paying the necessary ransom to obtain the prisoner or slave's release. The only adequate payment to redeem sinners from sin's slavery and its deserved punishment was the "precious blood of Christ" (1 Tim. 2:6; 1 Pet. 1:18–19), which was paid to God to satisfy His justice. Christ paid the ultimate price to free believers from bondage to sin.

UNLEASHING THE TEXT

Read 1:13–2:10, noting the key words and definitions next to the passage.

1 Peter 1:13–2:10 (NKJV)

gird up the loins of your mind (v. 13)—a word picture taken from the ancient practice of gathering up one's robes so as to be able to move in a hurry without tripping; here the metaphor is applied to one's thought process and conveys the need to carefully focus on God's future grace

be sober (v. 13)—spiritual steadfastness, self-control, clarity of mind, and moral decisiveness rather than intoxication by the world's allures

13 *Therefore gird up the loins of your mind, be sober, and rest your hope fully upon the grace that is to be brought to you at the revelation of Jesus Christ;*

14 *as obedient children, not conforming yourselves to the former lusts, as in your ignorance;*

15 *but as He who called you is holy, you also be holy in all your conduct,*

16 *because it is written, "Be holy, for I am holy."*

17 *And if you call on the Father, who without partiality judges according to each one's work, conduct yourselves throughout the time of your stay here in fear;*

18 *knowing that you were not redeemed with corruptible things, like silver or gold, from your*

aimless conduct received by tradition from your fathers,

19 but with the precious blood of Christ, as of a lamb without blemish and without spot.

20 He indeed was foreordained before the foundation of the world, but was manifest in these last times for you

21 who through Him believe in God, who raised Him from the dead and gave Him glory, so that your faith and hope are in God.

22 Since you have purified your souls in obeying the truth through the Spirit in sincere love of the brethren, love one another fervently with a pure heart,

23 having been born again, not of corruptible seed but incorruptible, through the word of God which lives and abides forever,

24 because "All flesh is as grass, and all the glory of man as the flower of the grass. The grass withers, and its flower falls away,

25 But the word of the LORD endures forever." Now this is the word which by the gospel was preached to you.

2:1 Therefore, laying aside all malice, all deceit, hypocrisy, envy, and all evil speaking,

2 as newborn babes, desire the pure milk of the word, that you may grow thereby,

3 if indeed you have tasted that the Lord is gracious.

4 Coming to Him as to a living stone, rejected indeed by men, but chosen by God and precious,

5 you also, as living stones, are being built up a spiritual house, a holy priesthood, to offer up spiritual sacrifices acceptable to God through Jesus Christ.

6 Therefore it is also contained in the Scripture, "Behold, I lay in Zion a chief cornerstone, elect, precious, and he who believes on Him will by no means be put to shame."

7 Therefore, to you who believe, He is precious; but to those who are disobedient, "The stone which the builders rejected has become the chief cornerstone,"

last times (v. 20)—the times of the Messiah, from His first advent to His second coming

love one another fervently (v. 22)—the love of choice (not sentimentality) that meets others at their point of need and stretches to the limits

not of corruptible seed (v. 23)—that is, the permanent, unfailing, supernatural spiritual life implanted by the Holy Spirit

desire the pure milk of the word (2:2)—Those with a new nature are marked by a craving for and delight in the truth of God.

Coming to Him (v. 4)—The Greek term connotes coming with the idea of remaining.

a living stone (v. 4)—an Old Testament phrase (see Isa. 8:14; 28:16; Ps. 118:22) that is both metaphor and paradox—a normal foundation is inanimate, but Christ is very much alive—the cornerstone of God's new "spiritual house"

built up a spiritual house (v. 5)—God is engineering an eternal entity, integrating His people into an organic whole.

A stone of stumbling . . . a rock of offense (v. 8)—Christ is either the means of salvation (to those who believe) or He is the means of judgment (to those who reject the gospel). He is like a stone in the road that causes a traveler to fall.

they also were appointed (v. 8)—not appointed to disobedience and unbelief but to doom because of their disobedience and unbelief

8 and "A stone of stumbling and a rock of offense."
   They stumble, being disobedient to the word, to
   which they also were appointed.

9 *But you are a chosen generation, a royal priesthood,*
   a holy nation, His own special people, that you may
   proclaim the praises of Him who called you out of
   darkness into His marvelous light;

10 *who once were not a people but are now the people*
   of God, who had not obtained mercy but now have
   obtained mercy.

a chosen generation (v. 9)—chosen for salvation

a royal priesthood (v. 9)—Israel temporarily forfeited its privileged calling to be a nation of priests. Presently, the church is fulfilling a priestly role in the world.

1) Under the inspiration of the Holy Spirit, Peter urges his readers to live holy lives. What reasons does he give?

_____

_____

_____

_____

(Verses to consider: Lev. 11:44–45; 18:30; 19:2; Matt. 5:48; Eph. 5:1)

2) This passage echoes the frequent New Testament command that believers must love one another (1:22). Describe the kind of love we are called to show to one another. Why is this important, especially in a situation like the one faced by Peter's original audience?

_____

_____

_____

_____

(Verses to consider: John 13:34; Rom. 12:10; Phil. 2:1–8; Heb. 13:1; 1 John 3:11)

3) How does this passage extol the power of the Word of God? What must be present in us before the Word can help us grow? What must we get rid of first before we can grow?

_____

_____

_____

_____

4) What truths from this passage encouraged Peter's audience to find their hope in their eternal blessings?

_____

_____

_____

_____

GOING DEEPER

Peter talks about "coming to [Christ] as to a living stone" (2:4). The Greek word translated *coming* means "to come with the idea of remaining." It conveys the idea of abiding with Christ in intimate fellowship. Compare that thought with the following words of Jesus. Read John 15:1–11.

1 *I am the true vine, and My Father is the vinedresser.*
2 *Every branch in Me that does not bear fruit He takes away; and every branch that bears fruit He prunes, that it may bear more fruit.*
3 *You are already clean because of the word which I have spoken to you.*
4 *Abide in Me, and I in you. As the branch cannot bear fruit of itself, unless it abides in the vine, neither can you, unless you abide in Me.*
5 *I am the vine, you are the branches. He who abides in Me, and I in him, bears much fruit; for without Me you can do nothing.*
6 *If anyone does not abide in Me, he is cast out as a branch and is withered; and they gather them and throw them into the fire, and they are burned.*
7 *If you abide in Me, and My words abide in you, you will ask what you desire, and it shall be done for you.*
8 *By this My Father is glorified, that you bear much fruit; so you will be My disciples.*
9 *As the Father loved Me, I also have loved you; abide in My love.*

10 *If you keep My commandments, you will abide in My love, just as I have kept My Father's commandments and abide in His love.*

11 *These things I have spoken to you, that My joy may remain in you, and that your joy may be full.*

Exploring the Meaning

5) What does it mean to abide in Christ? (Hint: What is an abode?)

_____

_____

_____

_____

6) Compare the image of Jesus as the vine with Peter's image of Jesus as a living stone. How are they alike? Different? What do they reveal about Christ?

_____

_____

_____

_____

7) How does abiding in Christ help a Christian living in a hostile world?

_____

_____

_____

_____

8) What is significant about the building terminology used in 1 Peter 2:4–8? What is God up to in the world? What is Christ's place in this cosmic plan? What is our role?

_____

_____

_____

_____

9) Peter charges his embattled readers to hunger for and crave God's Word. Why is this important? What are the benefits?

_____

_____

_____

_____

Truth for Today

A believer should count it a wasted day when he does not learn something new from or is not more deeply enriched by the truth of God's Word. Scripture is food for the believer's growth and power—and there is no other. The church today ignores the exposition and application of Scripture at its peril, as the warning of Hosea to Israel suggests: "My people are destroyed for lack of knowledge" (Hos. 4:6). The church cannot operate on truth it is not taught; believers cannot function on principles they have not learned. The most noble are still those who search the Scriptures daily (Acts 17:11).

Reflecting on the Text

10) What's your spiritual intake of God's Word? Are you malnourished, or are you experiencing a well-balanced diet of reading, hearing, studying, memorizing, and meditating upon Scripture? What needs to change this week?

_____

_____

_____

_____

(Verses to consider: Ps. 1:1–2; 19:7–11; 119:16, 24, 35, 37, 92, 97, 113, 127, 167, 174)

11) In a grand summary paragraph, Peter declares the calling of the church (2:9–10). How would you state his point in your own words? Are you living out this description? Why or why not?

_____

_____

_____

12) The mindset called for in this passage is one of being holy, sober minded, and having an eternal perspective. What activities tend to pull your thoughts away from the things of God and onto trivial issues? What do you need to do to focus more on eternal things?

_____

_____

_____

_____

Personal Response

Write out additional reflections, questions you may have, or a prayer.

_____

_____

_____

_____

_____

_____

_____

_____

_____

_____

_____

_____

_____

_____

_____

_____

_____

3

HONORABLE LIVING

1 Peter 2:11–3:12

DRAWING NEAR

How do you define the term "worldliness"? How can a Christian determine whether he or she is living in a worldly fashion?

_____

_____

_____

_____

Think of a Christian whom you would say lives honorably. Why do you say that? What about their life is honorable?

_____

_____

_____

_____

THE CONTEXT

With great apostolic wisdom and a tender shepherd's heart, the apostle Peter wrote this practical and encouraging epistle to beleaguered believers scattered across the Roman Empire. His message to them was, and is for us, one of hope. Despite temporal circumstances, believers have the wonderful and eternal blessing of salvation. In another apostle's words: "Eye has not seen, nor ear heard, nor have entered into the heart of man the things which God has prepared for those who love Him" (1 Cor. 2:9). In addition, believers, while living in a hostile world, have a holy obligation to proclaim the gospel and point others to Christ.

This passage focuses on honorable living by believers, before unbelievers (2:11–3:7) and before other believers (3:8–12). Christians are called to model humility and submission—both to the government, to masters (that is, on the job), and in the home. Such a lifestyle causes the world to stop, look, and wonder. Honorable living forces even unbelievers to acknowledge the greatness of our God!

21

Keys to the Text

Submission: To "submit" (2:13) is a military term meaning to subordinate oneself under another. No believer is inherently superior to any other believer. In their standing before God, they are equal in every way (Gal. 3:28). However, that does not diminish the importance of submission, for proper submission is a key theme of Spirit-filled living. The apostle Paul declared unequivocally that *every* Spirit-filled Christian is to be a humble, submissive Christian (Eph. 5:21). All believers must submit to each other; wives should submit to their husbands, children ought to submit to their parents (Eph. 6:1–3). Believers have to submit to government laws and ordinances (Rom. 13:1; 1 Pet. 2:13). Younger men need to submit to older men (1 Pet. 5:5a). *Every* believer is to be submissive in the ways God has ordained. In the matter of submission, our primary concern should not be about whom we should be *over* but whom we should be *under*. Humility will prevent the submitting person from becoming burdened, and the person submitted to from becoming overbearing.

Unleashing the Text

Read 2:11–3:12, noting the key words and definitions next to the passage.

sojourners and pilgrims (v. 11)—The Christian's true home is heaven.

abstain from fleshly lusts (v. 11)—Avoid all desires of the fallen nature (not just illicit sexual urges).

war against the soul (v. 11)—a picture of the destructive nature of sin

day of visitation (v. 12)—an Old Testament phrase that describes God's coming near either to judge or bless

silence . . . foolish men (v. 15)—Our obedience and humility shuts the mouths of those who are looking for reasons to criticize Christians.

liberty as a cloak for vice (v. 16)—Christian freedom is never to be an excuse for self-indulgence or license.

1 Peter 2:11–3:12 (NKJV)

11 *Beloved, I beg you as sojourners and pilgrims, abstain from fleshly lusts which war against the soul,*

12 *having your conduct honorable among the Gentiles, that when they speak against you as evildoers, they may, by your good works which they observe, glorify God in the day of visitation.*

13 *Therefore submit yourselves to every ordinance of man for the Lord's sake, whether to the king as supreme,*

14 *or to governors, as to those who are sent by him for the punishment of evildoers and for the praise of those who do good.*

15 *For this is the will of God, that by doing good you may put to silence the ignorance of foolish men—*

16 *as free, yet not using liberty as a cloak for vice, but as bondservants of God.*

17 Honor all people. Love the brotherhood. Fear God. Honor the king.

18 Servants, be submissive to your masters with all fear, not only to the good and gentle, but also to the harsh.

19 For this is commendable, if because of conscience toward God one endures grief, suffering wrongfully.

20 For what credit is it if, when you are beaten for your faults, you take it patiently? But when you do good and suffer, if you take it patiently, this is commendable before God.

21 For to this you were called, because Christ also suffered for us, leaving us an example, that you should follow His steps:

22 "Who committed no sin, nor was deceit found in His mouth";

23 who, when He was reviled, did not revile in return; when He suffered, He did not threaten, but committed Himself to Him who judges righteously;

24 who Himself bore our sins in His own body on the tree, that we, having died to sins, might live for righteousness—by whose stripes you were healed.

25 For you were like sheep going astray, but have now returned to the Shepherd and Overseer of your souls.

3:1 Wives, likewise, be submissive to your own husbands, that even if some do not obey the word, they, without a word, may be won by the conduct of their wives,

2 when they observe your chaste conduct accompanied by fear.

3 Do not let your adornment be merely outward—arranging the hair, wearing gold, or putting on fine apparel—

4 rather let it be the hidden person of the heart, with the incorruptible beauty of a gentle and quiet spirit, which is very precious in the sight of God.

5 For in this manner, in former times, the holy women who trusted in God also adorned themselves, being submissive to their own husbands,

honor (v. 17)—to demonstrate esteem that flows from inner respect

also to the harsh (v. 18)—Our submission is not contingent on the attitude or behavior of superiors.

to this you were called (v. 21)—Christians are sometimes called to suffer unjustly for their own maturity's sake and for the greater glory of God.

reviled (v. 23)—verbally abused

having died to sins, might live to righteousness (v. 24)—the miracle of being in Christ. That is, we were "in Him" when He died and when He rose, the result being that sin has no power over us and we now have the capacity to live holy lives.

Wives . . . be submissive (3:1)—Just as there is a God-ordained civil order, so there is a divine domestic order; neither implies any sense of superiority or inferiority.

won by the conduct of their wives (v. 1)—Loving, gracious submission is often the most powerful evangelistic tool a wife possesses.

outward (v. 3)—not a condemnation of external adornment but a warning against preoccupation with it

23

not afraid with any terror
(v. 6)—an encouragement to women who might naturally be anxious about submitting to an unbelieving husband

weaker vessel (v. 7)—Women are, by God's design, physically weaker and in need of protection, provision, and strength; thus husbands need to be attentive and responsive to their wives' needs, fears, and desires. Failure to do so can hinder a man's spiritual growth.

be of one mind (v. 8)—be likeminded or unified in heart

6 as Sarah obeyed Abraham, calling him lord, whose daughters you are if you do good and are not afraid with any terror.

7 Husbands, likewise, dwell with them with understanding, giving honor to the wife, as to the weaker vessel, and as being heirs together of the grace of life, that your prayers may not be hindered.

8 Finally, all of you be of one mind, having compassion for one another; love as brothers, be tenderhearted, be courteous;

9 not returning evil for evil or reviling for reviling, but on the contrary blessing, knowing that you were called to this, that you may inherit a blessing.

10 For "He who would love life and see good days, let him refrain his tongue from evil, and his lips from speaking deceit.

11 Let him turn away from evil and do good; let him seek peace and pursue it.

12 For the eyes of the LORD are on the righteous, and His ears are open to their prayers; but the face of the LORD is against those who do evil."

1) What kind of radically different conduct does Peter say is expected of believers (2:11–12)? What are "fleshly lusts"?

_____

_____

_____

2) As part of living honorably, Peter called for a lifestyle of submission. What does this word mean, and why does it cause such controversy in modern culture?

_____

_____

_____

(Verses to consider: Prov. 24:21; Jer. 29:4–14; Matt. 22:21; 1 Tim. 2:1)

3) What reasons does Peter give for submitting to governing authorities? What will happen when we do this?

_____

_____

_____

_____

_____

(Verses to consider: Rom. 13:1–7)

4) Peter talks about how Christ endured unjust suffering. How does Peter use that as an example of what it may mean for us to submit to an earthly master? How can we find encouragement from Christ's example?

_____

_____

_____

_____

_____

(Verses to consider: 1 Cor. 7:20–24; Eph. 6:5–7; Phil 2:5–11; Col. 3:22–25)

5) How does Peter describe what a wife's submission should look like? How can she do this? Why is this so important?

_____

_____

_____

_____

_____

6) What kind of relationship does Peter call husbands to cultivate with their wives? What does he say will happen if a husband fails to do this?

_____

_____

_____

_____

Going Deeper

Compare Peter's sobering charge with the apostle Paul's message to the Christians living in Rome. Read Romans 12:1–21.

1   *I beseech you therefore, brethren, by the mercies of God, that you present your bodies a living sacrifice, holy, acceptable to God, which is your reasonable service.*

2   *And do not be conformed to this world, but be transformed by the renewing of your mind, that you may prove what is that good and acceptable and perfect will of God.*

3   *For I say, through the grace given to me, to everyone who is among you, not to think of himself more highly than he ought to think, but to think soberly, as God has dealt to each one a measure of faith.*

4   *For as we have many members in one body, but all the members do not have the same function,*

5   *so we, being many, are one body in Christ, and individually members of one another.*

6   *Having then gifts differing according to the grace that is given to us, let us use them: if prophecy, let us prophesy in proportion to our faith;*

7   *or ministry, let us use it in our ministering; he who teaches, in teaching;*

8   *he who exhorts, in exhortation; he who gives, with liberality; he who leads, with diligence; he who shows mercy, with cheerfulness.*

9   *Let love be without hypocrisy. Abhor what is evil. Cling to what is good.*

10   *Be kindly affectionate to one another with brotherly love, in honor giving preference to one another;*

11   *not lagging in diligence, fervent in spirit, serving the Lord;*

12   *rejoicing in hope, patient in tribulation, continuing steadfastly in prayer;*

13   *distributing to the needs of the saints, given to hospitality.*

14   *Bless those who persecute you; bless and do not curse.*

15   *Rejoice with those who rejoice, and weep with those who weep.*

16   *Be of the same mind toward one another. Do not set your mind on high things, but associate with the humble. Do not be wise in your own opinion.*

17   *Repay no one evil for evil. Have regard for good things in the sight of all men.*

18   *If it is possible, as much as depends on you, live peaceably with all men.*

19   *Beloved, do not avenge yourselves, but rather give place to wrath; for it is written, "Vengeance is Mine, I will repay," says the Lord.*

20   *Therefore "If your enemy is hungry, feed him; if he is thirsty, give him a drink; for in so doing you will heap coals of fire on his head."*

21   *Do not be overcome by evil, but overcome evil with good.*

Exploring the Meaning

7) Romans 12 begins with a call for believers to have a renewed mind. In what ways is a new and different way of thinking necessary for living a radically different kind of life?

_____

_____

_____

_____

_____

8) Echoing much of what Peter wrote, what does Paul say are other marks of a loving, honorable life toward other Christians and non-Christians?

_____

_____

_____

_____

9) How do Peter's words call for Christian husbands to live differently in relationship to their wives (3:7)? How might obedience to these commands change the negative public perception of the notion of "submission" in marriage?

_____

_____

_____

_____

Truth for Today

The popular nineteenth-century English author William Arnot was described in this way: "His preaching is good. His writing is better. His living is best of all." That is the challenge. May it be said of all Christians that their living is best of all.

Reflecting on the Text

10) How is your living different and distinct? Do you blend in with the world or stand out from it? What issues of compromise or disobedience do you sense God wants you to deal with today?

_____

_____

_____

_____

11) How would you evaluate yourself in the area of submission (whether to government, an employer, or a spouse)? What are some specific behaviors you need to begin, or cease, in order to bring your life into line with Peter's words?

_____

_____

_____

_____

12) What two practical actions can you take this week to honor others? What friend can you ask to hold you accountable to do these things?

_____

_____

_____

_____

Personal Response

Write out additional reflections, questions you may have, or a prayer.

_____

_____

_____

_____

~ 4 ~
SUFFERING FOR GOOD

1 Peter 3:13–4:6

DRAWING NEAR

Some experts state that approximately 200 million Christians worldwide face the continual threat of harassment, torture, and even death because of their faith in Jesus Christ. It is believed that more followers of Christ were martyred in the twentieth century than in the previous nineteen centuries combined! Why do you think God allows His people to go through affliction and trial?

_____

_____

_____

_____

Have you been mistreated or made fun of for being a Christian, or for taking a stand for something good? What happened? How did you deal with it?

_____

_____

_____

_____

THE CONTEXT

Persecution of believers is not new nor should it be surprising. Jesus' final words to His disciples contain this sobering announcement: "And you will be hated by all for My name's sake. But he who endures to the end shall be saved" (Mark 13:13). This is not the kind of promise that most Christians embroider, frame, and hang above their dining room tables. Thus, believers must prepare for the inevitable. The entirety of 1 Peter is addressed to Christians living in a hostile culture. The thrust of the apostle's argument is that not only must believers endure persecution, but they also have a holy obligation to live honorably in the midst of their suffering. In this passage, Peter explains the principle and purpose of suffering for righteousness. Then he displays Christ as the paragon of what that means.

First Peter 3:13–4:6 is not a "feel good" passage. Nevertheless it was an urgent, needed reminder for first-century Christians. It is also an important message for us today, since we live in a time when the forces of evil are becoming more overt, more brazen, and more vicious than ever.

KEYS TO THE TEXT

Suffering: Agony, affliction, or distress; intense pain or sorrow. Suffering has been part of the human experience since people fell into sin (Gen. 3). The Bible makes it clear that some suffering results from evil action or sin in the world. But other times, suffering is forward-looking in that it serves to shape and refine God's children (1 Pet. 1:6–7; 5:10). The book of Hebrews declares that Jesus learned obedience by the things He suffered (Heb. 5:8), and that He was perfected through suffering (Heb. 2:10). Suffering has the potential of demonstrating God's power (2 Cor. 12:7). Those who suffer are in a position to comfort others (2 Cor. 1:3–6). Believers share in the suffering of Christ in the sense that through suffering they identify with Christ. To be a disciple involves suffering like the Master. Christ as Lord and His believers as disciples are bonded even further through the experience of suffering. (*Nelson's New Illustrated Bible Dictionary*)

Give a Defense: The English word *apologetics* comes from the Greek word here translated "defense." Using the word in an informal sense, Peter insists that the believer must understand what he believes and why he is a Christian, and then be able to articulate those beliefs humbly, thoughtfully, reasonably, and biblically.

UNLEASHING THE TEXT

Read 3:13–4:6, noting the key words and definitions next to the passage.

1 Peter 3:13–4:6 (NKJV)

blessed (v. 14)—"privileged" or "honored"

Sanctify the Lord God in your hearts (v. 15)—actually means to "set apart in your hearts Christ as Lord." The heart is the sanctuary in which He prefers to be worshiped. Live in submissive communion with the Lord Jesus, loving and obeying Him—and you have nothing to fear.

13 *And who is he who will harm you if you become followers of what is good?*

14 *But even if you should suffer for righteousness' sake, you are blessed. "And do not be afraid of their threats, nor be troubled."*

15 *But sanctify the Lord God in your hearts, and always be ready to give a defense to everyone who asks you a reason for the hope that is in you, with meekness and fear;*

16 *having a good conscience, that when they defame you as evildoers, those who revile your good conduct in Christ may be ashamed.*

17 *For it is better, if it is the will of God, to suffer for doing good than for doing evil.*

18 *For Christ also suffered once for sins, the just for the unjust, that He might bring us to God, being put to death in the flesh but made alive by the Spirit,*

19 *by whom also He went and preached to the spirits in prison,*

20 *who formerly were disobedient, when once the Divine longsuffering waited in the days of Noah, while the ark was being prepared, in which a few, that is, eight souls, were saved through water.*

21 *There is also an antitype which now saves us— baptism (not the removal of the filth of the flesh, but the answer of a good conscience toward God), through the resurrection of Jesus Christ,*

22 *who has gone into heaven and is at the right hand of God, angels and authorities and powers having been made subject to Him.*

4:1 *Therefore, since Christ suffered for us in the flesh, arm yourselves also with the same mind, for he who has suffered in the flesh has ceased from sin,*

a good conscience (v. 16)—A life free of ongoing and unconfessed sin will result in a clear conscience void of any sense of guilt.

For Christ also suffered (v. 18)—Not even Christ was exempt from suffering, and His faithful perseverance is a great example for every Christian.

once for sins (v. 18)—In contrast to the Old Covenant rituals of repeated sacrifices for sin, Christ offered Himself as the complete and final satisfaction for sin.

bring us to God (v. 18)—spiritually in this life, and fully in the next

preached (v. 19)—Between Christ's death and resurrection, His living spirit went to the demon spirits (that is, fallen angels) bound in the abyss, and He proclaimed that despite His death, He had triumphed over them.

disobedient . . . in the days of Noah (v. 20)—These bound demons had run amuck through the earth during the time of Noah, overstepping the bounds of God's tolerance. They had filled the world with their wicked, vile, anti-God activity, resulting in both its and their judgment.

saved through water (v. 20)—rescued despite the watery flood

an antitype which now saves us (v. 21)—In the New Testament, an antitype is an earthly expression of a spiritual reality; hence Noah's ark (with his family aboard, riding to safety) is analogous to Christians who are saved by being in "the ark of Christ."

baptism (v. 21)—This is not a reference to water baptism but to being brought into union with Christ. Following the analogy, remember that the occupants of Noah's ark were kept out of the water.

right hand of God (v. 22)—Christ was exalted to a place of prominence, honor, majesty, and power, after accomplishing His work on the cross and being raised from the dead.

the same mind (4:1)—Like their Master, Christians need to realize that one can be triumphant in suffering, even suffering to the point of death.

has ceased from sin (v. 1)—The worst that can happen to a suffering believer is that he or she suffers an unjust death; yet that is actually the best that can happen because death means the complete and final end of all sins!

lewdness (v. 3)—unbridled, unrestrained indulgence in sensual pleasure

revelries (v. 3)—orgies

they think it strange (v. 4)—Unbelievers do not understand and often resent the Christian's lack of interest in ungodly pleasures.

give an account (v. 5)—literally "to pay back" to God the debt of sin they have amassed

to those who are dead (v. 6)—Peter had in mind believers who had heard and accepted the gospel when they were still alive, but who had died before he wrote this letter.

2 *that he no longer should live the rest of his time in the flesh for the lusts of men, but for the will of God.*

3 *For we have spent enough of our past lifetime in doing the will of the Gentiles—when we walked in lewdness, lusts, drunkenness, revelries, drinking parties, and abominable idolatries.*

4 *In regard to these, they think it strange that you do not run with them in the same flood of dissipation, speaking evil of you.*

5 *They will give an account to Him who is ready to judge the living and the dead.*

6 *For this reason the gospel was preached also to those who are dead, that they might be judged according to men in the flesh, but live according to God in the spirit.*

1) What did Peter urge believers to do in the face of suffering (3:15)? What does this mean? How does one do this?

_____

_____

_____

_____

_____

2) What kind of suffering is blessed (3:14, 16–17)? Why?

_____

_____

_____

_____

_____

3) Peter portrays Christ as the ultimate example of enduring suffering. In what ways was His suffering different from the mistreatment we receive? In what ways is our "suffering for righteousness' sake" (3:14) similar to Christ's suffering?

_____

_____

_____

_____

(Verses to consider: Heb. 7:26–27; 9:26–28)

4) Peter uses the story of Noah as an antitype—an earthly expression of a spiritual reality—to illustrate how Christ's suffering on our behalf enables believers to be safely carried through God's judgment against sin. What theological insights do you gain from this passage (3:18–22)?

_____

_____

_____

_____

(Verses to consider: 2 Pet. 2:4–5; Jude 6–7; Gen. 6:1–8)

Going Deeper

Read about the sufferings of the apostle Paul in 2 Corinthians 11:22–33.

22 *Are they Hebrews? So am I. Are they Israelites? So am I. Are they the seed of Abraham? So am I.*

23 *Are they ministers of Christ?—I speak as a fool—I am more: in labors more abundant, in stripes above measure, in prisons more frequently, in deaths often.*

24 *From the Jews five times I received forty stripes minus one.*

25 *Three times I was beaten with rods; once I was stoned; three times I was shipwrecked; a night and a day I have been in the deep;*

26 *in journeys often, in perils of waters, in perils of robbers, in perils of my own countrymen, in perils of the Gentiles, in perils in the city, in perils in the wilderness, in perils in the sea, in perils among false brethren;*

27 *in weariness and toil, in sleeplessness often, in hunger and thirst, in fastings often, in cold and nakedness—*

28 *besides the other things, what comes upon me daily: my deep concern for all the churches.*

29 *Who is weak, and I am not weak? Who is made to stumble, and I do not burn with indignation?*

30 *If I must boast, I will boast in the things which concern my infirmity.*

31 *The God and Father of our Lord Jesus Christ, who is blessed forever, knows that I am not lying.*

32 *In Damascus the governor, under Aretas the king, was guarding the city of the Damascenes with a garrison, desiring to arrest me;*

33 *but I was let down in a basket through a window in the wall, and escaped from his hands.*

EXPLORING THE MEANING

5) Why was Paul experiencing so many trials?

_____

_____

_____

_____

6) Put yourself in Paul's shoes. How do you think he felt at some of the low points mentioned in the above passage?

_____

_____

_____

_____

7) How does a Christian maintain an eternal perspective when suffering for doing good?

_____

_____

_____

_____

Truth for Today

Persecution quickly burns away chaff in the church. Those who have made only a superficial profession of Christ have no new nature to motivate them to suffer for Christ and no divine power to enable them to endure it if they wanted to. Nothing is more spiritually purifying and strengthening than persecution (see James 1:12).

Reflecting on the Text

8) Think of a time when you have been "persecuted" recently for doing good or for what you believe. How has it had a strengthening affect on your faith?

_____

_____

_____

_____

9) Peter talks about having the "same mind" toward suffering as Jesus had in His suffering (1 Pet. 4:1–2). How can Jesus' example help you when you face trials?

_____

_____

_____

_____

10) This passage explains that those who persecute others will not have the last laugh. A day of reckoning approaches. In what way(s) does this motivate you to be faithful?

_____

_____

_____

_____

(Verses to consider: Rev. 20:11–15; Rom. 3:19; 2 Thess. 1:6–10)

11) If someone this week asked, "Why are you a Christian?" what would you say? How can you be ready to give a reason for the hope that you have in Christ?

_____

_____

_____

_____

PERSONAL RESPONSE

Write out additional reflections, questions you may have, or a prayer.

_____

_____

_____

_____

_____

_____

_____

_____

_____

_____

_____

_____

_____

_____

_____

_____

_____

~ 5 ~
PRAY, LOVE, SERVE

DRAWING NEAR

Peter continues his letter by urging us to live for God and love each other. Do you consider yourself a loving person? Why or why not?

_____

_____

_____

When you hear someone say, "The end of the world is near," how do you usually respond? Why?

_____

_____

_____

THE CONTEXT

Having emphasized triumphant suffering, perhaps that leads to death, Peter begins to emphasize triumphant suffering with the "end" in mind, which is the second coming of Christ. He is calling believers to live obediently and expectantly in the light of Christ's return. Peter is reminding the readers of this letter that the return of Jesus Christ could be at any moment, so they should be serious and watchful, maintaining a proper eternal perspective on life. Peter utilized the persecution of his Christian brothers to wake them up to some of the great truths of the Christian faith:

- This world is not all there is.
- This world is not the believer's home.
- Believers have a guaranteed future that is too wonderful for words.
- Believers have a unique opportunity to serve each other and tell others about Christ.

Keys to the Text

Fervent Love: The word *fervent* means "to be stretched, to be strained." It is used of a runner moving at maximum output with taut muscles straining and stretching to the limit (1 Pet. 1:22). This kind of love requires the Christian to put another's spiritual good ahead of his own desires in spite of being treated unkindly, ungraciously, or even with hostility (1 Cor. 13:4–7; Phil. 2:1–4).

Spiritual Gifts: The Greek word for *spiritual* literally means "pertaining to the Spirit," referring to that which has spiritual qualities or characteristics or is under some form of spiritual control. The word *gifts* comes from the Greek word *charisma* and means essentially "gift of grace" or "free gift"; in sixteen of its seventeen New Testament uses it is connected to God as the Giver. Spiritual gifts are divine enablements for ministry that the Holy Spirit gives in some measure to all believers. These are to be completely under His control and used for the building of the church to Christ's glory.

Unleashing the Text

Read 4:7–11, noting the key words and definitions next to the passage.

1 Peter 4:7–11 (NKJV)

the end of all things (v. 7)—not a chronological termination, but a consummation or achieving of God's goal

is at hand (v. 7)—is imminent; that is, could be at any moment

be serious and watchful (v. 7)—a command to not be carried away by passions or emotions but, rather, to have an eternal perspective in this life

7 But the end of all things is at hand; therefore be serious and watchful in your prayers.

8 And above all things have fervent love for one another, for "love will cover a multitude of sins."

9 Be hospitable to one another without grumbling.

10 As each one has received a gift, minister it to one another, as good stewards of the manifold grace of God.

"love will cover a multitude of sins" (v. 8)—a quote from Proverbs 10:12. It is the nature of true spiritual love, whether from God to man or Christian to Christian, to cover sins (cf. Rom. 5:8). This teaching does not preclude the discipline of a sinning, unrepentant church member (cf. Matt. 18:15–18; 1 Cor. 5). It means specifically that a Christian should overlook sins against him if possible, and always be ready to forgive insults and unkindnesses.

Be hospitable (v. 9)—The Greek word means "love of strangers" and meant, practically, to open one's home to travelers and strangers.

received a gift (v. 10)—Every believer has something to contribute.

minister it to one another (v. 10)—Gifts are to be used to benefit and serve others, not to enhance one's own position or prestige.

good stewards (v. 10)—A steward manages the resources of another, meaning that our gifts do not belong to us; rather, they are on loan from God.

11 *If anyone speaks, let him speak as the oracles of God. If anyone ministers, let him do it as with the ability which God supplies, that in all things God may be glorified through Jesus Christ, to whom belong the glory and the dominion forever and ever. Amen.*

speaks . . . ministers (v. 11)—This implies that there are two categories of gifts: speaking gifts and serving gifts.

oracles of God (v. 11)—the very words out of God's mouth

God may be glorified (v. 11)—the goal of everything

1) Why does Peter charge his readers to be serious and watchful in prayer?

_____

_____

_____

_____

_____

(Verses to consider: Rom. 13:12; 1 Thess. 1:10; James 5:7–8; Rev. 22:20)

2) What kind of love does Peter command believers to demonstrate? What is the difference between "covering over" sin and excusing sin?

_____

_____

_____

_____

_____

(Verses to consider: Prov. 10:12; Matt. 18:15–17; 1 Cor. 5)

3) What does biblical hospitality look like?

_____

_____

_____

_____

_____

(Verses to consider: Gen. 18:1–8; Deut. 14:28–29; 1 Tim. 3:2)

4) What fact about spiritual gifts does Peter assume to be true?

_____

_____

_____

_____

_____

GOING DEEPER

For more insight about how we should love other members of the body of Christ, read 1 Corinthians 13:1–13.

1   *Though I speak with the tongues of men and of angels, but have not love, I have become sounding brass or a clanging cymbal.*

2   *And though I have the gift of prophecy, and understand all mysteries and all knowledge, and though I have all faith, so that I could remove mountains, but have not love, I am nothing.*

3   *And though I bestow all my goods to feed the poor, and though I give my body to be burned, but have not love, it profits me nothing.*

4   *Love suffers long and is kind; love does not envy; love does not parade itself, is not puffed up;*

5   *does not behave rudely, does not seek its own, is not provoked, thinks no evil;*

6   *does not rejoice in iniquity, but rejoices in the truth;*

7   *bears all things, believes all things, hopes all things, endures all things.*

8   *Love never fails. But whether there are prophecies, they will fail; whether there are tongues, they will cease; whether there is knowledge, it will vanish away.*

9   *For we know in part and we prophesy in part.*

10 *But when that which is perfect has come, then that which is in part will be done away.*

11 *When I was a child, I spoke as a child, I understood as a child, I thought as a child; but when I became a man, I put away childish things.*

12 *For now we see in a mirror, dimly, but then face to face. Now I know in part, but then I shall know just as I also am known.*

13 *And now abide faith, hope, love, these three; but the greatest of these is love.*

Exploring the Meaning

5) Why is love greater than faith and hope?

_____

_____

_____

_____

6) What are some misconceptions about love in our culture? How do these wrong ideas compare with the description of love in 1 Corinthians 13?

_____

_____

_____

_____

_____

7) Read 1 John 4:7–21. What extra insights does this passage give you into your Christian obligation to love others?

_____

_____

_____

_____

Truth for Today

The doctrine of the imminent return of Christ should lead the believer into a watchful pursuit of holiness. Moreover, a watchful attitude creates a pilgrim mentality (2:11). It reminds the Christian that he is a citizen of heaven only sojourning on earth. It should also remind him that he will face the record of his service to God and be rewarded for what stands the test at the judgment seat of Christ, which follows the return of Christ to rapture His church. . . . Not to use our [spiritual] gift is an affront to God's wisdom, a rebuff of His love and grace, and a loss to His church. We did not determine our gift, deserve it, or earn it. But we all have a gift from the Lord, and if we do not use it, His work is weakened and His heart is grieved.

Reflecting on the Text

8) The text reminds us that life on earth is brief and that we should focus on eternal realities. Why is this so difficult? How can the promises of the next world motivate us to live rightly in this one?

_____

_____

_____

_____

(Verses to consider: 1 Cor. 3:10–15; 4:1–5; 2 Cor. 5:9–10)

9) Which aspects of love as described here do you struggle with the most? Why?

_____

_____

_____

_____

10) Peter twice refers to the glory that God deserves. How should the "glory of God" figure into a believer's daily activities and schedule?

_____

_____

_____

_____

11) Name some practical ways you can use your gifts this week to live more fully for the glory of God.

_____

_____

_____

_____

Personal Response

Write out additional reflections, questions you may have, or a prayer.

_____

_____

_____

_____

_____

_____

_____

_____

_____

_____

_____

_____

_____

_____

_____

_____

_____

_____

_____

_____

_____

_____

_____

_____

_____

_____

_____

_____

_____

ADDITIONAL NOTES

JOY EVEN IN SUFFERING

1 Peter 4:12–19

DRAWING NEAR

The church is under siege in most cultures of the world, especially in what is now called the two-thirds world. What is most amazing about the suffering of our brothers and sisters worldwide is the way they continue to serve the Lord with tremendous joy and zeal. In many of these places, the church is actually thriving and flourishing! How do you explain this? How is it that those who suffer for the name of Christ can endure it with joy?

_____

_____

_____

_____

How do you tend to respond to the daily difficulties in your life? Check the ways that apply to you.

_____ grumbling

_____ trying to fix it

_____ discouragement

_____ faith in God's plan

_____ questioning, why me?

_____ worry and anxiety

_____ joy

THE CONTEXT

In good times, the church seems to become stagnant and complacent. In hard times, the church seems to grow and be strengthened. Why is that? Whatever the reason, there's something about difficulty and trial that forces us to look beyond the superficial and trivial to the things that matter most. C. S. Lewis once observed, "God whispers to us in our pleasures, speaks in our conscience, but shouts in our pains: it is His megaphone to rouse a deaf world."

Writing to beleaguered believers across the Roman Empire, the apostle urged them to live with joy, hope and purity, even in the face of terrible trials.

Peter was no stranger to suffering, so he writes from experience and reiterates the unique perspective Christians can have in the midst of trials. This passage presents four attitudes necessary for triumphal living: Christians should expect persecution (and not be surprised by it); Christians should rejoice in the midst of difficulty; Christians should evaluate the cause of suffering; and Christians should entrust their lives to God.

Keys to the Text

Joy: This means to exult and rejoice with a rapturous joy. Joy is not the natural human response to trouble. Christians are under divine command to be more than *somewhat* joyful in their trials; they are called to look upon them with *all* joy. Peter speaks of a unique fullness of joy that the Lord graciously provides His children when they willingly endure troubles while trusting in Him—regardless of the cause, type, or severity of the distress. God will always use them for our benefit and for His own glory. Not because of some sort of religious masochism, but rather because of a sincere trust in the promise and goodness of our Lord, we can look on trials as a welcome friend. Like Joseph, we can know that what others may have meant for evil against us, God means for good (Gen. 50:20; cf. Rom. 8:28).

Unleashing the Text

Read 4:12–19, noting the key words and definitions next to the passage.

1 Peter 4:12–19 (NKJV)

the fiery trial (v. 12)—Peter is believed to have written this letter at about the time of the burning of Rome and at the beginning of a two-hundred-year period of Christian persecution.

12 Beloved, do not think it strange concerning the fiery trial which is to try you, as though some strange thing happened to you;

13 but rejoice to the extent that you partake of Christ's sufferings, that when His glory is revealed, you may also be glad with exceeding joy.

some strange thing happened (v. 12)—"Happened" means "to fall by chance"; Christians must not think that persecution is an accident. God allows it and designs it for the believer's testing, purging, and cleansing.

partake of Christ's sufferings (v. 13)—When believers are persecuted for doing what is right, they enjoy a special camaraderie with Christ.

when His glory is revealed (v. 13)—Though He is presently glorified in heaven, Christ's full glory will not be revealed on earth until the Second Coming.

be glad with exceeding joy (v. 13)—Exult and rejoice with rapturous joy, knowing that your reward is certain.

14 *If you are reproached for the name of Christ, blessed are you, for the Spirit of glory and of God rests upon you. On their part He is blasphemed, but on your part He is glorified.*

15 *But let none of you suffer as a murderer, a thief, an evildoer, or as a busybody in other people's matters.*

16 *Yet if anyone suffers as a Christian, let him not be ashamed, but let him glorify God in this matter.*

17 *For the time has come for judgment to begin at the house of God; and if it begins with us first, what will be the end of those who do not obey the gospel of God?*

18 *Now "If the righteous one is scarcely saved, where will the ungodly and the sinner appear?"*

19 *Therefore let those who suffer according to the will of God commit their souls to Him in doing good, as to a faithful Creator.*

reproached for the name of Christ (v. 14)—insulted and mistreated because of one's commitment to and association with Jesus

blessed (v. 14)—specific benefit, not a general, nondescript happiness

rests upon you (v. 14)—God's presence rests upon and strengthens believers who are suffering.

busybody in other people's matters (v. 15)—This is a command to not get involved in revolutionary or disruptive activity either in one's workplace or in dealing with governing authorities.

Christian (v. 16)—Originally a term of derision, this label came to be loved and adopted by followers of Jesus.

judgment . . . house of God (v. 17)—not condemnation, but purging, chastening, and purifying of the church by the loving hand of God

commit their souls to Him (v. 19)—a banking term meaning "to deposit for safe keeping"

faithful Creator (v. 19)—As Creator, God knows best the needs of His beloved creatures.

1) What does this passage say about the inevitability of suffering for Christians? Is it normal or not? Why?

_____

_____

_____

_____

(Verses to consider: Matt. 5:10–12; Gal. 6:17; Phil. 1:29; 3:10; Col. 1:24)

2) What does it mean to partake of Christ's suffering?

_____

_____

_____

3) Peter mentions the possibility of glorifying God in the midst of suffering. How is this possible?

_____

_____

_____

_____

4) What does Peter mean by saying that "judgment . . . begins at the house of God" (v. 17)?

_____

_____

_____

_____

GOING DEEPER

James, a leader in the early church, also wrote about suffering and faith. Look for further insights in James 1:2–6.

2 *My brethren, count it all joy when you fall into various trials,*
3 *knowing that the testing of your faith produces patience.*
4 *But let patience have its perfect work, that you may be perfect and complete, lacking nothing.*
5 *If any of you lacks wisdom, let him ask of God, who gives to all liberally and without reproach, and it will be given to him.*
6 *But let him ask in faith, with no doubting, for he who doubts is like a wave of the sea driven and tossed by the wind.*

EXPLORING THE MEANING

5) What does it mean to count all trials as joy?

_____

_____

_____

_____

6) What, according to James, are some "positive" results of suffering?

_____

_____

_____

_____

_____

7) Read 2 Corinthians 12:7–10. What was Paul's experience of Christ in the midst of great suffering?

_____

_____

_____

_____

_____

Truth for Today

A pure, powerful church will inevitably provoke a hostile reaction from the satanic world system. Successful Christians and churches will make waves, and the world and Satan will retaliate with persecution. God has always used suffering to perfect and purify His people and to demonstrate the sufficiency of His grace. It's only when we don't trust in His sovereignty or don't understand His purposes that we are apt to experience worry, fear, and anxiety when things go wrong. But suffering brings enormous benefits.

Reflecting on the Text

8) What benefits have you received from going through a time of suffering? In what ways have you experienced God's supportive grace in tough times?

_____

_____

_____

_____

_____

9) How can you improve your "joy quotient" in times of suffering? How can trusting God lead to real joy?

_____

_____

_____

_____

10) Peter encouraged his persecuted brethren to "commit their souls" to their "faithful Creator." Explain what this means as though you were giving encouragement to a friend who was going through suffering.

_____

_____

_____

_____

11) What sobers you most as you consider the truths taught in this passage? What encourages you most? Why?

_____

_____

_____

_____

PERSONAL RESPONSE

Write out additional reflections, questions you may have, or a prayer.

_____

_____

_____

_____

_____

_____

_____

7

REQUIREMENTS FOR LEADERSHIP

DRAWING NEAR

Think of a Christian leader (that is, a pastor, youth director, Sunday-school teacher, and so forth) who has had a lasting impact on your life. What outstanding qualities did they possess? How did God use them in your life?

_____

_____

_____

_____

_____

THE CONTEXT

In the first four chapters Peter addressed the church as a whole, stressing not only the future inheritance that awaits believers in heaven but also their present calling to be a "royal priesthood" and a "holy nation" in the midst of a corrupt culture. By living humble, submissive, and pure lives, by modeling love for one another, and by patiently enduring suffering, the believers would glorify God and also be salt and light in a dark world.

In the final chapter of his letter, Peter addresses the leaders of the struggling church. Times of suffering and persecution call for the noblest leadership. Those who shepherd God's flock, then and now, have unique responsibilities that should never be taken lightly.

KEYS TO THE TEXT

Elders: An elder is the same as a "shepherd" (that is, "pastor") and "overseer" (that is, "bishop"). In the New Testament, the words _bishop, elder, overseer,_ and _pastor_ are used interchangeably to describe the same men. Elders are responsible to lead, preach and teach, help the spiritually weak, care for the church, and ordain other leaders. The word emphasizes spiritual maturity, and the plural indicates the need for a plurality of leaders to oversee and shepherd God's flock.

Unleashing the Text

Read 5:1–4, noting the key words and definitions next to the passage.

1 Peter 5:1–4 (NKJV)

I exhort (v. 1)—Peter motivated these leaders in several ways: (1) by referring to himself as a fellow-elder (hence, he would be experienced and qualified to give relevant exhortation); (2) by appealing to his apostolic authority as an eyewitness of Christ's sufferings; (3) by reminding them of the reward they would one day receive in exchange for their faithful service.

partaker of the glory (v. 1)—a reference to Peter's experience observing the transfiguration of Christ

1 *The elders who are among you I exhort, I who am a fellow elder and a witness of the sufferings of Christ, and also a partaker of the glory that will be revealed:*

2 *Shepherd the flock of God which is among you, serving as overseers, not by compulsion but willingly, not for dishonest gain but eagerly;*

3 *nor as being lords over those entrusted to you, but being examples to the flock;*

4 *and when the Chief Shepherd appears, you will receive the crown of glory that does not fade away.*

Shepherd the flock (v. 2)—A primary role of a shepherd is to feed the sheep (thus God's leaders must be able to teach); another is to protect the flock.

of God (v. 2)—The flock belongs to God, not to the pastor.

not by compulsion, but willingly (v. 2)—a warning against laziness and indifference

not for dishonest gain (v. 2)—a warning to not be like the false teachers (so prevalent in every era) who are motivated primarily by financial gain

nor as being lords (v. 3)—God-honoring leaders will not attempt to use their position to dominate others, to intimidate, or to manipulate situations.

Chief Shepherd appears (v. 4)—a reminder that pastors will be evaluated at the Judgment Seat of Christ

crown of glory (v. 4)—literally, the crown which is eternal glory; a symbol of victorious achievement and perseverance, granted to the faithful

1) How does Peter describe himself in verse 1? Why?

_____

_____

_____

_____

_____

_____

2) Peter raises the issue of a pastor's motivation. What are the some of the wrong reasons to "shepherd the flock" of God's people?

_____

_____

_____

_____

_____

3) What are the right motivations to serve as a shepherd?

_____

_____

_____

_____

_____

4) How can a congregation help its leader(s) avoid the temptations cited in this passage?

_____

_____

_____

_____

_____

(Verses to consider: Titus 1:7–9; 1 Tim. 5:17–20)

5) Some churches cite Ephesians 4:11–12 to say full-time, vocational pastors should not be put on a pedestal; rather that all of God's people should strive to set an example to the rest. What do you think about this?

_____

_____

_____

_____

_____

Going Deeper

Read the following passage from 1 Timothy 3:1–13, and compare its advice to leaders to that of Peter's in chapter 5.

1   *This is a faithful saying: If a man desires the position of a bishop, he desires a good work.*

2   *A bishop then must be blameless, the husband of one wife, temperate, sober-minded, of good behavior, hospitable, able to teach;*

3   *not given to wine, not violent, not greedy for money, but gentle, not quarrelsome, not covetous;*

4   *one who rules his own house well, having his children in submission with all reverence*

5   *(for if a man does not know how to rule his own house, how will he take care of the church of God?);*

6   *not a novice, lest being puffed up with pride he fall into the same condemnation as the devil.*

7   *Moreover he must have a good testimony among those who are outside, lest he fall into reproach and the snare of the devil.*

8   *Likewise deacons must be reverent, not double-tongued, not given to much wine, not greedy for money,*

9   *holding the mystery of the faith with a pure conscience.*

10 *But let these also first be tested; then let them serve as deacons, being found blameless.*

11 *Likewise, their wives must be reverent, not slanderers, temperate, faithful in all things.*

12 *Let deacons be the husbands of one wife, ruling their children and their own houses well.*

13 *For those who have served well as deacons obtain for themselves a good standing and great boldness in the faith which is in Christ Jesus.*

Exploring the Meaning

6) Why does God give such stringent standards for leadership? Can anyone really live up to these requirements? Should public/civil leaders be held to the same standards? Why or why not?

_____

_____

_____

7) Read Matthew 20:25–28. What warning did Jesus give His disciples about leadership in the church?

_____

_____

_____

_____

_____

8) What does it mean that Jesus is the "Chief Shepherd" (1 Pet. 5:4)?

_____

_____

_____

_____

_____

_____

(Verses to consider: Isa. 40:11; Zech. 13:7; John 10:2–5, 11–16)

TRUTH FOR TODAY

Some judge the success of a servant of God by how large or widespread his ministry is, how many degrees he has, or how much publicity he receives. But the true measure of a servant of God is whether he focuses solely on pleasing God, which gives him the willingness to serve with humility and suffer opposition from those hostile to the truth.

REFLECTING ON THE TEXT

9) This passage mentions "the crown of glory." To what does this refer? How does a Christian merit such a reward?

_____

_____

_____

_____

(Verses to consider: 1 Cor. 9:24–25; James 1:12; 2 Tim. 4:8; 1 Thess. 2:19)

10) Do you think it is easy or difficult to lead a church body? Would you want to trade places with your pastor? Why or why not?

_____

_____

_____

_____

11) In what two or three tangible ways will you encourage your pastor(s) this week and demonstrate support for their ministry?

_____

_____

_____

_____

PERSONAL RESPONSE

Write out additional reflections, questions you may have, or a prayer.

_____

_____

_____

_____

_____

_____

_____

_____

_____

_____

8

CHRISTIAN VICTORY

DRAWING NEAR

As Peter ends this letter, he assures the readers of their final victory but warns them to watch out for Satan's attacks. Do you think Satan is real? Why or why not?

_____

_____

_____

_____

How do you define "humility"? Why is it such a rare commodity today, even in the church?

_____

_____

_____

_____

THE CONTEXT

Put yourself in the situation faced by first-century Christians living in the part of the Roman Empire known as Asia. You heard wonderful news about the one true God sending His own Son into the world to save people from their sins. This Jesus of Nazareth was executed on a Roman cross but three days later rose from the dead! Then He went back to heaven with the promise to return one day soon for those who love Him. You embraced this message and found a joy and peace that you had never known. But friends, neighbors, government officials, and even family members became antagonistic and began to criticize and harass you. Then the persecution turned violent. You huddle secretly with other discouraged Christian friends. You are scared and confused. If God is all-powerful, and if this gospel is true, why the intense suffering?

One day a letter arrives. It is from Peter, an eyewitness of the life, death, and resurrection of Jesus and a fearless leader of the church, one who understands firsthand what it means to suffer. Peter's words are filled with hope and promise.

He reminds you that this world is not your home and that God has called you to something higher and deeper and greater. You can endure. You will have victory. And as you submit to God's eternal purposes with humility and trust, you have a unique opportunity to bring honor and glory before a watching world to the One who has saved you.

Peter reminds us that God will, through it all, "perfect, establish, strengthen, and settle [us]." That is why we can exultantly proclaim, "To Him be the glory and the dominion forever and ever. Amen."

KEYS TO THE TEXT

Humility: The word used here literally means "lowly-mindedness," an attitude that one is not too good to serve. Humility was not considered a virtue by the ancient world, any more than it is today. The opposite of humility would be conceit and the pursuit of personal glory, which is the motivation for selfish ambition. The basic definition of true humility is to "esteem others better than himself" (Phil. 2:3). Christ provides the ultimate example of selfless humility (Matt. 11:29; John 13:12–17).

UNLEASHING THE TEXT

Read 5:5–14, noting the key words and definitions next to the passage.

1 Peter 5:5–14 (NKJV)

5 *Likewise you younger people, submit yourselves to your elders. Yes, all of you be submissive to one another, and be clothed with humility, for "God resists the proud, but gives grace to the humble."*

6 *Therefore humble yourselves under the mighty hand of God, that He may exalt you in due time,*

7 *casting all your care upon Him, for He cares for you.*

elders (v. 5)—pastors and other spiritual leaders of the church. Church members (especially those young in the faith) are to give honor, deference, and respect to their spiritual leaders.

be clothed with humility (v. 5)—To "be clothed" means to tie something on oneself with a knot or a bow. This term was often used of a slave putting on an apron over his clothes in order to keep his clothes clean.

under the mighty hand of God (v. 6)—an Old Testament symbol of the power of God working in human experience. To be impatient with God in His work of humbling believers is to demonstrate a lack of submission and humility.

exalt you in due time (v. 6)—God will lift up the suffering, submissive believers in His wisely appointed time.

casting all your care upon Him (v. 7)—literally, to throw one's discontent, discouragement, and despair onto the Lord with confidence that He knows what He is doing

8 Be sober, be vigilant; because your adversary the devil walks about like a roaring lion, seeking whom he may devour.

9 Resist him, steadfast in the faith, knowing that the same sufferings are experienced by your brotherhood in the world.

10 But may the God of all grace, who called us to His eternal glory by Christ Jesus, after you have suffered a while, perfect, establish, strengthen, and settle you.

11 To Him be the glory and the dominion forever and ever. Amen.

12 By Silvanus, our faithful brother as I consider him, I have written to you briefly, exhorting and testifying that this is the true grace of God in which you stand.

13 She who is in Babylon, elect together with you, greets you; and so does Mark my son.

14 Greet one another with a kiss of love. Peace to you all who are in Christ Jesus. Amen.

Be sober (v. 8)—the clarity of mind to resist worldly allurements and to have an eternal perspective

be vigilant (v. 8)—Be alert, careful, wary, mindful of the strategies of the evil one.

your adversary (v. 8)—Greek for an opponent in a court of law

a roaring lion (v. 8)—a picture of Satan's vicious, malevolent nature. He wants to destroy believers.

Resist him, steadfast in the faith (v. 9)—Believers are to stand up against the devil, by remaining firm in the Christian faith (that is, living according to Scripture).

after you have suffered a while (v. 10)—God's purposes realized in the future require some pain in the present.

perfect, establish, strengthen, and settle (v. 10)—strength and resoluteness of character that God is building into His people through their suffering

Silvanus (v. 12)—Silas, a Roman citizen (Acts 16:37) and Paul's frequent traveling companion

Babylon (v. 13)—a veiled reference to Rome (see Introduction)

1) Why is submission to church leaders an important practice for the church, especially for the younger members?

_____

_____

_____

_____

_____

_____

(Verses to consider: 1 Cor. 16:15–16; 1 Thess. 5:12–13; Titus 3:1–2; Heb. 13:7, 17)

2) According to Peter, what is involved in exhibiting true humility?

_____

_____

_____

_____

(Verses to consider: John 13:3–17; Phil. 2:3–4; Prov. 6:16–17)

3) How does Peter describe the devil here? What is the Christian's defense against this diabolical enemy?

_____

_____

_____

_____

(Verses to consider: Luke 22:3; John 13:27; 2 Cor. 4:3–4; Rev. 12:10)

4) What do you learn about God from this passage? What actions and attributes of His are noted?

_____

_____

_____

_____

GOING DEEPER

To get a fresh reminder of the ultimate victory that is yours in Christ, read Revelation 20:10–21:8.

> **20:10** *The devil, who deceived them, was cast into the lake of fire and brimstone where the beast and the false prophet are. And they will be tormented day and night forever and ever.*
>
> **11** *Then I saw a great white throne and Him who sat on it, from whose face the earth and the heaven fled away. And there was found no place for them.*

12 *And I saw the dead, small and great, standing before God, and books were opened. And another book was opened, which is the Book of Life. And the dead were judged according to their works, by the things which were written in the books.*

13 *The sea gave up the dead who were in it, and Death and Hades delivered up the dead who were in them. And they were judged, each one according to his works.*

14 *Then Death and Hades were cast into the lake of fire. This is the second death.*

15 *And anyone not found written in the Book of Life was cast into the lake of fire.*

21:1 *Now I saw a new heaven and a new earth, for the first heaven and the first earth had passed away. Also there was no more sea.*

2 *Then I, John, saw the holy city, New Jerusalem, coming down out of heaven from God, prepared as a bride adorned for her husband.*

3 *And I heard a loud voice from heaven saying, "Behold, the tabernacle of God is with men, and He will dwell with them, and they shall be His people. God Himself will be with them and be their God.*

4 *And God will wipe away every tear from their eyes; there shall be no more death, nor sorrow, nor crying. There shall be no more pain, for the former things have passed away."*

5 *Then He who sat on the throne said, "Behold, I make all things new." And He said to me, "Write, for these words are true and faithful."*

6 *And He said to me, "It is done! I am the Alpha and the Omega, the Beginning and the End. I will give of the fountain of the water of life freely to him who thirsts.*

7 *He who overcomes shall inherit all things, and I will be his God and he shall be My son.*

8 *But the cowardly, unbelieving, abominable, murderers, sexually immoral, sorcerers, idolaters, and all liars shall have their part in the lake which burns with fire and brimstone, which is the second death."*

EXPLORING THE MEANING

5) How does John describe in greater detail the "eternal glory" of heaven?

_____

_____

_____

6) What is Satan's final end? How does this fact encourage you to live victoriously today?

_____

_____

_____

_____

7) In what way does the future hope of Revelation 20:3–4 relate to Peter's command to cast your cares upon God?

_____

_____

_____

_____

Truth for Today

A guard who sees the enemy approaching does not run out and start fighting. He reports the attack to his commanding officer, who then organizes the defense. When Satan attacks, it is foolish to try to do battle with him alone. Like the soldier on guard duty, we should simply report to the Commander and leave the defense in His hands.

Reflecting on the Text

8) In what specific areas of life do you face Satan's attack most severely and repeatedly? How are you faring? What could you do differently today to better resist him?

_____

_____

_____

_____

9) Review the four things Peter prayed for his Christian friends who were being persecuted (v. 10). What do these terms imply? In what ways do you need these qualities?

_____

_____

_____

_____

10) What would it look like (in practical, down-to-earth terms) for you today to "humble yourself under the mighty hand of God, that He may exalt you in due time"?

_____

_____

_____

_____

Personal Response

Write out additional reflections, questions you may have, or a prayer.

_____

_____

_____

_____

_____

_____

_____

_____

_____

ADDITIONAL NOTES

Introduction to 2 Peter

The clear claim in 1:1 to authorship by the apostle Peter gives the epistle its title. To distinguish it from Peter's first epistle, it was given the Greek title "Petrou B," or 2 Peter.

Author and Date

The author of 2 Peter is the apostle Peter (see Introduction to 1 Peter). The very first verse makes that claim; 3:1 refers to his first letter; 1:14 refers to the Lord's prediction of Peter's death (John 21:18–19); 1:16–18 mentions being at the Transfiguration (Matt. 17:1–4). Despite this evidence, critics have generated more controversy over 2 Peter's authorship and rightful place in the canon of Scripture than over any other New Testament book. The church fathers were slow in giving it their acceptance. In fact, no church father refers to 2 Peter by name until Origen near the beginning of the third century. The ancient church historian, Eusebius, only included 2 Peter in his list of disputed books, along with James, Jude, 2 John, and 3 John. Even the leading Reformers only hesitatingly accepted it.

The question about differences in Greek style between the two letters has been satisfactorily answered. In 1 Peter 5:12, Peter wrote that he used an amanuensis, Silvanus. In this second letter, Peter either used a different amanuensis or wrote the letter himself.

The differences in vocabulary between the two letters can be explained by the differences in themes. First Peter was written to help suffering Christians. Second Peter was written to expose false teachers. On the other hand, the two books contain remarkable similarities in their vocabulary. The salutation, "grace and peace be multiplied to you," is essentially the same in both. And the author uses such words as "precious," "virtue," "putting off," and "eyewitness" in both letters. Certain rather unusual words found in 2 Peter are also found in Peter's speeches in the Acts of the Apostles. These include "obtained" (1:1; Acts 1:17); "godliness" (1:3, 6–7; 3:11; Acts 3:12); and "wages of unrighteousness" (2:13, 15; Acts 1:18). Both letters also refer to the same Old Testament event (2:5; 1 Pet. 3:18–20). Some scholars have pointed out that there are as many similarities in vocabulary between 1 and 2 Peter as there are between 1 Timothy and Titus, two letters almost universally believed to have been written by Paul.

The difference in themes explains certain emphases, such as why one letter teaches that the Second Coming is near, and one deals with its delay. First Peter, ministering especially to suffering Christians, focuses on the imminency of Christ as a means of encouraging the Christians. Second Peter, dealing with scoffers, emphasizes the reasons why that imminent return of Christ has not yet occurred. Other proposed differences invented by the critics, such as the contradiction between including the resurrection of Christ in one letter and the Transfiguration of Christ in the other, seem to be contrived.

Moreover, it is seemingly irrational that a false teacher would spuriously write a letter against false teachers. No unusual, new, or false doctrines appear in this epistle. So, if 2 Peter were a forgery, it would be a forgery written by a fool for no reason at all. This is too much to believe. The conclusion to the question of authorship is that, when the writer introduced the letter and referred to himself as Peter, he was writing the truth.

Nero died in AD 68, and tradition says Peter died in Nero's persecution. The epistle may have been written just before his death (1:14; ca. AD 67–68).

Background and Setting

Since the time of writing and sending his first letter, Peter had become increasingly concerned about false teachers who were infiltrating the churches in Asia Minor. Though these false teachers had already caused trouble, Peter expected that their heretical doctrines and immoral lifestyles would result in more damage in the future. Thus Peter, in what was almost his last will and testament (1:13–15), wrote to warn the beloved believers in Christ about the doctrinal dangers they would face.

Peter does not explicitly say where he was when he wrote this letter, as he does in 1 Peter (1 Pet. 5:13). But the consensus seems to be that Peter wrote this letter from prison in Rome, where he was facing imminent death. Shortly after this letter was written, Peter was martyred, according to reliable tradition, by being crucified upside down.

Peter says nothing in the salutation about the recipients of this letter. But according to 3:2, Peter was writing another epistle to the same people to whom he wrote 1 Peter. In his first letter, he spelled out that he was writing "to the pilgrims of the Dispersion in Pontus, Galatia, Cappadocia, Asia, and Bithynia" (1 Pet. 1:1). These provinces were located in an area of Asia Minor, which is modern Turkey. The Christians to whom Peter wrote were mostly Gentiles (see note on 1:1).

Historical and Theological Themes

Second Peter was written to expose, thwart, and defeat false teachers who were invading the church. Peter intended to instruct Christians in how to defend themselves against these false teachers and their deceptive lies. This book is the most graphic and penetrating exposé of false teachers in Scripture, comparable only to Jude.

Other themes for this letter can be discerned in the midst of Peter's polemic against the false teachers. He wanted to motivate his readers to continue to develop their Christian character (1:5–11). In so doing, he explains wonderfully how a believer can have assurance of his or her salvation. Peter also wanted to persuade his readers of the divine character of the apostolic writings (1:12–21). Near the end of the letter, he presents reasons for the delay in Christ's second coming (3:1–13).

Another recurring theme is the importance of knowledge. Some form of the word "knowledge" appears 16 times in these three short chapters. It is not too much to say that Peter's primary solution to false teaching is knowledge of true doctrine. Other distinctive features of 2 Peter include a precise statement on the divine origin of Scripture (1:20–21); the future destruction of the world by fire (3:8–13); and the recognition of Paul's letters as inspired Scripture (3:15–16).

INTERPRETIVE CHALLENGES

Perhaps the most important challenge in the epistle is to rightly interpret 1:19–21 because of its far-reaching implications with regard to the nature and authenticity of Scripture. That passage, along with 2 Timothy 3:15–17, is vital to a sound view of the Bible's inspiration. Peter's remark that the Lord "bought" false teachers (2:1) poses a challenge, interpretively and theologically, with regard to the nature of the atonement. The identity of the angels who sinned (2:4) also challenges the interpreter. Many who believe that the saved can be lost again use 2:18–22 for their argument. That passage, directed at false teachers, must be clarified so as not to contradict a similar statement to believers in 1:4. Further, whom does God not want to perish (3:9)? All of these matters will be treated in the notes.

Notes

~9~
KNOW YOUR SALVATION

2 Peter 1:1–11

DRAWING NEAR

Peter begins his second book by talking about being diligent to grow in the knowledge of God. Consider your own "spiritual knowledge." On a scale of 1 to 10, with 1 being "spiritual simpleton" and 10 being "Bible scholar," how would you rate yourself?

_____

_____

_____

Are you secure in your salvation? Why or why not?

_____

_____

_____

_____

THE CONTEXT

The churches of Asia Minor faced a growing problem. Numerous false teachers had infiltrated their group and were teaching dangerous, false doctrines. Apparently, some in the church were embracing these heresies, prompting the apostle to write this stern condemnation of all who would lead God's people astray. More than a jeremiad against wolf-like teachers, however, this letter is a warning to the church. In fact, the message of this brief epistle says that the best way to defend against spiritual error is to *know the truth*.

Consequently, in his opening paragraphs, Peter counseled the flock of God in Asia Minor to take pains to grasp the full implications of their salvation. Specifically, those believers needed to be reminded that their salvation was sustained by God's power (1:3–4), that it was confirmed by fruitful growth in the faith (1:5–7), and that it would eventually result in honor and abundant reward (1:8–11). Because false teachers and heretical doctrines continue to flourish today, we need to hear, understand, and heed the warnings of 2 Peter.

Keys to the Text

Knowledge: "Knowledge" is a key word in 2 Peter (vv. 2, 5, 6, 8; 2:20; 3:18). Throughout Scripture, it implies an intimate knowledge (Amos 3:2), and is even used for sexual intercourse (Gen. 4:1). Peter doesn't emphasize a superficial knowledge, or a mere surface awareness of the facts about Christ, but a genuine, personal sharing of life with Christ, based on repentance from sin and personal faith in Him. This is a strengthened form of "knowledge," implying a larger, more thorough, and intimate knowledge. The Christian's precious faith is built on knowing the truth about God. Christianity is not a mystical religion, but is based in objective, historical, revealed, rational truth from God and is intended to be understood and believed. The deeper and wider that knowledge of the Lord, the more "grace and peace" are multiplied in the believer.

Godliness: To be godly is to live reverently, loyally, and obediently toward God. Peter means that the genuine believer ought not to ask God for something more (as if something necessary to sustain his growth, strength, and perseverance was missing) to become godly, because he already has every spiritual resource to manifest, sustain, and perfect godly living.

Unleashing the Text

Read 1:1–11, noting the key words and definitions next to the passage.

2 Peter 1:1–11 (NKJV)

a bondservant and apostle (v. 1)—a balance of humility and dignity, so important for those who would serve Christ and His church

to those (v. 1)—The audience for this letter is the same as for 1 Peter.

obtained (v. 1)—probably means "attained by divine will"; in other words, by grace and not human effort

1 *Simon Peter, a bondservant and apostle of Jesus Christ, to those who have obtained like precious faith with us by the righteousness of our God and Savior Jesus Christ:*

2 *Grace and peace be multiplied to you in the knowledge of God and of Jesus our Lord,*

3 *as His divine power has given to us all things that*

like precious (v. 1)—All Christians, both "high" and "low", have received the same priceless, saving faith; there are no first- and second-class believers.

faith (v. 1)—the Christian's power to believe; a gift granted by God

by the righteousness (v. 1)—All Christians share in salvation only because of the righteousness imputed to them by God.

our God and Savior Jesus Christ (v. 1)—a clear statement of Christ's deity

His divine power (v. 3)—Christ's power is the source of the believer's sufficiency and perseverance.

pertain to life and godliness, through the knowledge of Him who called us by glory and virtue,

4 by which have been given to us exceedingly great and precious promises, that through these you may be partakers of the divine nature, having escaped the corruption that is in the world through lust.

5 But also for this very reason, giving all diligence, add to your faith virtue, to virtue knowledge,

6 to knowledge self-control, to self-control perseverance, to perseverance godliness,

7 to godliness brotherly kindness, and to brotherly kindness love.

8 For if these things are yours and abound, you will be neither barren nor unfruitful in the knowledge of our Lord Jesus Christ.

9 For he who lacks these things is shortsighted, even to blindness, and has forgotten that he was cleansed from his old sins.

10 Therefore, brethren, be even more diligent to make your call and election sure, for if you do these things you will never stumble;

11 for so an entrance will be supplied to you abundantly into the everlasting kingdom of our Lord and Savior Jesus Christ.

called us by glory and virtue (v. 3)—God's call to salvation requires that sinners understand Christ's revealed majesty and moral excellence as the only Lord and Savior.

partakers of the divine nature (v. 4)—At conversion, Christians do not become little gods, but they are regenerated; that is, they become "new creations" by virtue of having been born again into Christ.

escaped the corruption (v. 4)—At the time of salvation, believers are freed from the power that the rottenness in the world has over them through their fallen, sinful nature.

giving all diligence (v. 5)—In light of all of God's blessings, the Christian must be totally dedicated and make a maximum effort to live for God.

add to your faith (v. 5)—to supply lavishly. Believers are to add their full and complete devotion to the marvelous faith and grace given first by God.

virtue (v. 5)—moral excellence demonstrated outwardly and powerfully in life

self-control (v. 6)—literally, "hold oneself in"; to exercise self-restraint and self-discipline

perseverance (v. 6)—patient endurance in doing right

brotherly kindness (v. 7)—affection for others that is willing to sacrifice

barren (v. 8)—inactive, indolent, and useless

unfruitful (v. 8)—unproductive

shortsighted, even to blindness (v. 9)—A professing Christian who is missing the virtues mentioned above is unable to discern his or her true spiritual condition and thus can have no assurance of his or her salvation.

make your call and election sure (v. 10)—Though God is "sure" who His elect are and has given them an eternally secure salvation, the Christian might not always have assurance of this salvation, unless he or she pursues the spiritual qualities cited by Peter.

stumble (v. 10)—into fear and doubt as a result of an unproductive life

abundantly into the everlasting kingdom (v. 11)—A rich entrance into heavenly reward is the hope and reality for every believer who lives a faithful, fruitful life here on earth.

1) Peter begins by talking about the power of Christ. Why is this an important starting point? What does Christ's power do for believers?

_____

_____

_____

_____

_____

(Verses to consider: Matt. 24:30; Mark 5:30; Luke 4:14; 5:17; Rom. 1:4; 2 Cor. 12:9)

2) What does "partakers of the divine nature" mean? What does it not mean?

_____

_____

_____

_____

_____

(Verses to consider: John 3:3; James 1:18; 1 Pet. 1:23;
Rom. 8:1, 9; John 1:12; Gal. 2:20; 2 Cor. 5:17)

3) What role does human effort play in the Christian life (vv. 5–9)?

_____

_____

_____

_____

(Verses to consider: Phil. 2:12–13; Col. 1:28–29)

4) Describe the results Peter says will come through diligently growing in faith and in the knowledge of the Lord.

_____

_____

_____

_____

_____

GOING DEEPER

Consider what Romans 8:31–39 says about the Christian's eternal security.

31 *What then shall we say to these things? If God is for us, who can be against us?*

32 *He who did not spare His own Son, but delivered Him up for us all, how shall He not with Him also freely give us all things?*

33 *Who shall bring a charge against God's elect? It is God who justifies.*

34 *Who is he who condemns? It is Christ who died, and furthermore is also risen, who is even at the right hand of God, who also makes intercession for us.*

35 *Who shall separate us from the love of Christ? Shall tribulation, or distress, or persecution, or famine, or nakedness, or peril, or sword?*

36 *As it is written: "For Your sake we are killed all day long; we are accounted as sheep for the slaughter."*

37 *Yet in all these things we are more than conquerors through Him who loved us.*

38 *For I am persuaded that neither death nor life, nor angels nor principalities nor powers, nor things present nor things to come,*

39 *nor height nor depth, nor any other created thing, shall be able to separate us from the love of God which is in Christ Jesus our Lord.*

EXPLORING THE MEANING

5) According to this passage, is the Christian's calling to salvation a sure thing? What factors can threaten or jeopardize a person's salvation?

Righteousness Love & Truth

(Verses to consider: John 10:27–29; 1 Pet. 1:1–5)

73

6) If salvation and God's eternal love are assured to the true believer, then why do so many Christians lack assurance? How does an unfruitful life aggravate these feelings of doubt?

_____

_____

_____

_____

_____

(Verses to consider: Matt. 13:22; James 2:20–22)

7) What popular current philosophies or false teachings in our culture and in the church create problems for immature Christians who are not grounded in the faith?

_____

_____

_____

_____

_____

_____

TRUTH FOR TODAY

A tragic defect in much contemporary evangelism is the reliance on syllogistic assurance. A person making a profession of faith in Jesus Christ is presented with the following syllogism, designed to provide assurance of salvation: "Those who put their faith in Jesus Christ will be saved. You have put your faith in Him. Therefore, you are saved." Unfortunately, the second premise presupposes that the individual's faith is genuine, which cannot be proven at that moment but can be proved by his perseverance. The result of such defective evangelistic methodology is that many who do not have genuine faith are given a false psychological assurance. Genuine biblical assurance is God's gift through the Holy Spirit to obedient believers.

Reflecting on the Text

8) What in your life demonstrates that you have become a "partaker of the divine nature"? In other words, what evidence is there that you are "a new creation" in Christ and that "all things have become new" (2 Cor. 5:17)?

---

9) From the list of things to "add to your faith" (1:5–9), what areas do you need to grow in? What will you do this week to begin?

---

10) What primary lesson is God trying to teach you through this passage? Why do you think that?

PERSONAL RESPONSE

Write out additional reflections, questions you may have, or a prayer.

KNOW YOUR SCRIPTURES

DRAWING NEAR

You get into a spiritual conversation with an unchurched neighbor who has no clear religious beliefs. When you make reference to the Bible, he or she says: "Wait a minute! You keep quoting the Bible, but how do I know that what it says is true? I mean, the Mormons believe the Book of Mormon. The Muslims have the Koran. What makes the Bible so special? It's just a bunch of stories and myths, right?" What would you say?

_____

_____

_____

_____

Why do you believe the Bible is true?

_____

_____

_____

_____

_____

THE CONTEXT

Writing to Christians who were being inundated by false teachers spouting dangerous doctrines, Peter, the aged apostle, emphasized the importance of knowing (and living by) the truth. But how does one differentiate between the claims of one person and the claims of another? According to this passage, the Old Testament (and, by implication, the New Testament) Scriptures are completely authoritative and trustworthy for two reasons: they were certified by apostolic witnesses, and they were inspired not by human whims but by the miraculous leading of the Holy Spirit.

Because the concept of truth is under attack these days, this is an important passage for Christians to understand and apply.

Keys to the Text

Inspiration of Scripture: Both Old and New Testaments are included in the "Scriptures," and are given by God. The word *inspired* means literally "breathed out by God," or "God-breathed." Sometimes God told the Bible writers the exact words to say (e.g., Jer. 1:9), but more often He used their minds, vocabularies, and experiences to produce His own perfect infallible, inerrant Word. It is important to note that inspiration applies only to the original autographs of Scripture, not the Bible writers; there are no inspired Scripture writers, only inspired Scripture.

Unleashing the Text

Read 1:12–21, noting the key words and definitions next to the passage.

2 Peter 1:12–21 (NKJV)

will not be negligent (v. 12)—Truth always needs repetition because believers forget so easily.

tent (v. 13)—Death is described as laying aside one's tent.

shortly (v. 14)—Peter was probably in his seventies as he wrote this letter (likely from a Roman prison), and he anticipated dying in the near future. According to tradition, he was crucified upside down, refusing to be crucified in the same way as his Lord.

Christ showed me (v. 14)—Christ had prophesied the death Peter would die almost forty years previously.

that you always have a reminder ... after my decease (v. 15)—Peter's inspired letter would be a permanent record for God's people.

12 For this reason I will not be negligent to remind you always of these things, though you know and are established in the present truth.

13 Yes, I think it is right, as long as I am in this tent, to stir you up by reminding you,

14 knowing that shortly I must put off my tent, just as our Lord Jesus Christ showed me.

15 Moreover I will be careful to ensure that you always have a reminder of these things after my decease.

16 For we did not follow cunningly devised fables when we made known to you the power and coming of our Lord Jesus Christ, but were eyewitnesses of His majesty.

17 For He received from God the Father honor and glory when such a voice came to Him from the Excellent Glory: "This is My beloved Son, in whom I am well pleased."

cunningly devised fables (v. 16)—mythical stories about gods and miracles. Such tales were often concocted by false teachers to gain followers, wealth, and power.

made known (v. 16)—revealed something previously hidden

eyewitnesses of His majesty (v. 16)—a broad reference to Christ's life, ministry, and resurrection; probably also a reference to Peter's presence at the Transfiguration, where all of Christ's kingdom splendor was briefly revealed

Excellent Glory (v. 17)—a reference to the glory cloud on the Mount of Transfiguration

18 *And we heard this voice which came from heaven when we were with Him on the holy mountain.*

19 *And so we have the prophetic word confirmed, which you do well to heed as a light that shines in a dark place, until the day dawns and the morning star rises in your hearts;*

20 *knowing this first, that no prophecy of Scripture is of any private interpretation,*

21 *for prophecy never came by the will of man, but holy men of God spoke as they were moved by the Holy Spirit.*

when we were with Him (v. 18)—Peter, James, and John had seen the preview of Christ's kingdom and glory and thus were to be believed over the false teachers.

the prophetic word confirmed (v. 19)—The Greek word order is important here; the sentence could be rendered "we have more sure the prophetic word." The idea is that the "prophetic word" (that is, Scripture) is a more complete, more permanent, more reliable, more authoritative testimony than anyone's personal experience, however genuine the person may be.

you do well to heed (v. 19)—Believers who are exposed to false teachings need to cling to the truth of inspired Scripture.

the day dawns and the morning star rises (v. 19)—God's Word is a lamp that shines in the darkness of this world until the second coming of Christ when the perfect but limited revelation of the written Word of God will give way to the perfect and complete revelation of the living Word of God.

prophecy of Scripture (v. 20)—a reference to all of the Old Testament and, by implication, all of the New Testament

private interpretation (v. 20)—The Greek word translated "interpretation" has the idea of loosing; thus, the idea is that no Scripture is the result of a human being "untying" or "loosing" their own ideas.

by the will of man (v. 21)—Scripture was never produced as a result of a person's decision.

moved by the Holy Spirit (v. 21)—The writers of Scripture were literally "carried along" or "borne along" by the will of the Spirit of God.

1) Peter seemed to be keenly aware that his days on earth were numbered. In light of his impending death, what was his great concern (vv. 12–15)?

_____

_____

_____

_____

_____

_____

_____

2) What is Peter referring to when he talks about "fables" (v. 16)? What accusations is he making? What accusations is he likely facing? How does that tie in with his subsequent teaching about Scripture?

_____

_____

_____

_____

_____

_____

(Verses to consider: 1 Tim. 1:3–4; 4:7; 2 Tim. 4:5; Titus 1:13–14; Ps. 119:105; John 17:17)

3) Peter cites his own experience with briefly seeing the glory of Christ. Why is this significant to his argument here?

_____

_____

_____

_____

_____

_____

(Verses to consider: Matt. 16:28; 17:1–8)

GOING DEEPER

Second Timothy 3:14–17 contains an important passage about the authenticity and reliability of Scripture.

14 *But you must continue in the things which you have learned and been assured of, knowing from whom you have learned them,*

15 *and that from childhood you have known the Holy Scriptures, which are able to make you wise for salvation through faith which is in Christ Jesus.*

16 *All Scripture is given by inspiration of God, and is profitable for doctrine, for reproof, for correction, for instruction in righteousness,*

17 *that the man of God may be complete, thoroughly equipped for every good work.*

EXPLORING THE MEANING

4) Compare Paul's discussion of Scripture written to his protégé, Timothy, with Peter's teaching. What is similar? What is new?

_____

_____

_____

_____

5) What insights does Paul give into the origin and purpose of Scripture?

_____

_____

_____

_____

6) Paul speaks of Scripture as being given by inspiration. Peter talks of the writers being "moved" or carried along by the Spirit. What does this mean? What do these words and phrases imply?

_____

_____

_____

_____

(Verses to consider: Luke 1:70; Jer. 1:4; Rom. 3:2; 1 Cor. 2:10)

7) "Inerrancy" is the doctrine stating that God, through the Holy Spirit, superintended the human authors of Scripture so that, using their own individual personalities, thought processes, and vocabulary, they composed and recorded without error the exact words God wanted written. What does this doctrine have to say to those who argue that the Bible is God's literal dictation to the world? What does this say to those who claim the Bible is just a human-made book?

_____

_____

_____

(Verses to consider: Prov. 30:5; John 10:34–35; 17:17; 1 Cor. 14:36–37)

TRUTH FOR TODAY

The argument is proposed that Scripture is but a collection of various men's ideas about God and about right and wrong. One person's interpretation of the Bible is therefore just as good as another's, and there is no place for dogmatism. Men have been left free to believe or not believe, to follow or not follow, any or all of the Scripture as it suits them. Each person becomes his own judge over Scripture, and the end result is to disregard it altogether. It is impossible, however, to take Jesus seriously and not take Scripture seriously. It is impossible to believe that Jesus spoke absolute truth and not to consider Scripture to be that absolute truth because that is precisely what Jesus taught it to be. If Jesus was mistaken or deluded on this point, there would be no reason to accept anything else that He said. At the outset of His ministry He makes clear that His authority and Scripture's authority are the same; His truth and Scripture's truth are identical and inseparable.

REFLECTING ON THE TEXT

8) Peter's realization of the limited time left to him on earth prompted him to give his full energy and attention to eternal matters. What about you? How are you spending your time? If you knew your time was short, what would you do differently? Why?

_____

_____

_____

_____

_____

9) What false teachings or "fables" do you see people indulging and believing in? What can you do to confront them?

_____

_____

_____

_____

_____

10) What new insight or truth have you gained into the nature of God's Word? What will you begin doing differently as a result?

_____

_____

_____

_____

_____

_____

_____

PERSONAL RESPONSE

Write out additional reflections, questions you may have, or a prayer.

_____

_____

_____

_____

_____

_____

_____

_____

_____

_____

_____

_____

_____

ADDITIONAL NOTES

KNOW YOUR ADVERSARIES

DRAWING NEAR

What are some of the more common and dangerous examples of "false teaching"—according to Scripture—that are popular where you live? What makes them so popular?

_____

_____

_____

How do you discern what is true and what is false? How do you determine what teaching you will listen to and what teaching you will reject?

_____

_____

_____

THE CONTEXT

The main impetus for this letter was the growing number of false teachers in the church. Peter wanted believers to be able to discern these deceivers. Though Peter identifies no specific individual, cult, or teaching, he shows how to determine whether heresy is being taught. False teachers are deceptive in their infiltration (2:1–3), doomed by their iniquity (2:4–10a), disdainful in their impurity (2:10b–17), and devastating in their impact (2:18–22).

Second Peter 2 is relevant for us today as well, because some contemporary teachers and self-proclaimed experts also make remarkable claims about themselves and their teachings. This chapter is a textbook lesson on learning how to discern and defeat heresy.

KEYS TO THE TEXT

False Teachers: Peter described false teachers in detail in this chapter so that Christians would always recognize their characteristics and methods. The description of the false teachers is somewhat generic. Peter does not identify any specific false religion, cult, or system of teaching. In a general characterization of false teachers, he informs us that they teach destructive heresies. They deny Christ and twist the Scriptures. They bring true faith into dispute. And they mock the second coming of Christ. But Peter was just as concerned with showing the immoral character of these teachers as he was with exposing their teaching. Thus, he describes them in more detail than he describes their doctrines. Wickedness is not the product of sound doctrine but of "destructive heresies" (2:1). The greatest sin of Christ-rejecters and the most damning work of Satan is misrepresentation of the truth and its consequent deception. Nothing is more wicked than for someone to claim to speak for God to the salvation of souls when in reality he speaks for Satan to the damnation of souls.

Unleashing the Text

Read 2:1–22, noting the key words and definitions next to the passage.

2 Peter 2:1–22 (NKJV)

among the people (v. 1)—Satan has always endeavored to infiltrate groups of believers with deception.

destructive heresies (v. 1)—"Destructive" means leading to ultimate damnation; "heresies" means self-designed religious lies; the combination is sobering.

denying the Lord who bought them (v. 1)—denying His sovereign lordship, His right to rule their lives, despite claiming to be His followers

many will follow (v. 2)—These teachers will successfully recruit vast numbers of nominal believers.

the way of truth will be blasphemed (v. 2)—The world mocks and scoffs at hypocrites.

their judgment . . . does not slumber (v. 3)—God, in His perfect time, will act against these liars and deceivers.

the angels who sinned (v. 4)—Apparently, this is a reference to the fallen angels of Genesis 6 who left their normal state and lusted after women.

cast . . . and delivered . . . to be reserved (v. 4)—the deepest pit of hell where some angels are being incarcerated until their final consignment to the lake of fire

did not spare the ancient world (v. 5)—a reference to the worldwide flood of Noah's day

1 But there were also false prophets among the people, even as there will be false teachers among you, who will secretly bring in destructive heresies, even denying the Lord who bought them, and bring on themselves swift destruction.

2 And many will follow their destructive ways, because of whom the way of truth will be blasphemed.

3 By covetousness they will exploit you with deceptive words; for a long time their judgment has not been idle, and their destruction does not slumber.

4 For if God did not spare the angels who sinned, but cast them down to hell and delivered them into chains of darkness, to be reserved for judgment;

5 and did not spare the ancient world, but saved Noah, one of eight people, a preacher of righteousness, bringing in the flood on the world of the ungodly;

6 *and turning the cities of Sodom and Gomorrah into ashes, condemned them to destruction, making them an example to those who afterward would live ungodly;*

7 *and delivered righteous Lot, who was oppressed by the filthy conduct of the wicked*

8 *(for that righteous man, dwelling among them, tormented his righteous soul from day to day by seeing and hearing their lawless deeds)—*

9 *then the Lord knows how to deliver the godly out of temptations and to reserve the unjust under punishment for the day of judgment,*

10 *and especially those who walk according to the flesh in the lust of uncleanness and despise authority. They are presumptuous, self-willed. They are not afraid to speak evil of dignitaries,*

11 *whereas angels, who are greater in power and might, do not bring a reviling accusation against them before the Lord.*

12 *But these, like natural brute beasts made to be caught and destroyed, speak evil of the things they do not understand, and will utterly perish in their own corruption,*

13 *and will receive the wages of unrighteousness, as those who count it pleasure to carouse in the daytime. They are spots and blemishes, carousing in their own deceptions while they feast with you,*

14 *having eyes full of adultery and that cannot cease from sin, enticing unstable souls. They have a heart trained in covetous practices, and are accursed children.*

15 *They have forsaken the right way and gone astray, following the way of Balaam the son of Beor, who loved the wages of unrighteousness;*

Sodom and Gomorrah (v. 6)—another ancient example of the truth that wickedness results in judgment

righteous Lot (vv. 7–8)—Lot had spiritual weaknesses, but righteousness was imputed to him, as it is to all the saved, by faith in the true God.

to deliver the godly out of temptations (v. 9)—that is, from destructive attacks

to reserve the unjust (v. 9)—The wicked are kept like prisoners awaiting their final sentencing.

despise authority (v. 10)—The false teachers identified with Christ outwardly but would not submit to His lordship.

angels, who are greater in power (v. 11)—holy angels who have more power than humans

do not bring a reviling accusation (v. 11)—Holy angels so revere the Lord that they dare not speak insults against any authority.

utterly perish (v. 12)—False teachers cannot get beyond their own instincts and thus will be destroyed by the folly of those passions.

carouse in the daytime (v. 13)—Sinning without the cover of darkness was indicative of their wide-open, brazen perversity.

spots and blemishes (v. 13)—dirty blotches, scabs—the antithesis of the character of Christ

enticing unstable souls (v. 14)—a fishing metaphor; literally, to beguile or catch with bait

heart trained in covetous practices (v. 14)—The false teachers had trained, prepared, and equipped their minds to focus on what was forbidden.

Balaam (v. 15)—an Old Testament compromising prophet for sale to whomever paid him, who preferred wealth and popularity over faithfulness and obedience to God

16 *but he was rebuked for his iniquity: a dumb donkey speaking with a man's voice restrained the madness of the prophet.*

17 *These are wells without water, clouds carried by a tempest, for whom is reserved the blackness of darkness forever.*

18 *For when they speak great swelling words of emptiness, they allure through the lusts of the flesh, through lewdness, the ones who have actually escaped from those who live in error.*

19 *While they promise them liberty, they themselves are slaves of corruption; for by whom a person is overcome, by him also he is brought into bondage.*

20 *For if, after they have escaped the pollutions of the world through the knowledge of the Lord and Savior Jesus Christ, they are again entangled in them and overcome, the latter end is worse for them than the beginning.*

21 *For it would have been better for them not to have known the way of righteousness, than having known it, to turn from the holy commandment delivered to them.*

22 *But it has happened to them according to the true proverb: "A dog returns to his own vomit," and, "a sow, having washed, to her wallowing in the mire."*

wells . . . clouds (v. 17)—False teachers operate under the pretense of being able to quench the spiritual thirsts of souls; they have nothing to give.

great swelling words of emptiness (v. 18)—high-sounding words that masquerade as scholarship or profound insights

escaped the pollutions of the world (v. 20)—"Pollutions" conveys the idea of putrid or poisonous vapors; the world gives off a deadly influence.

to turn from the holy commandment (v. 21)—to "turn back"; a reference to the perversion and defection of the false teachers

1) Peter notes that false teachers are not new. What does he suggest as these people's motives?

_____

_____

_____

_____

_____

_____

(Verses to consider: Deut. 13:1–18; Jer. 23; Ezek. 13; Gal. 3:1; 2 Tim. 4:3–4)

2) How does Peter describe these false teachers? What adjectives does he use? What word pictures? These false teachers may have looked good on the outside, but what does Peter say was really going on underneath their spiritual front?

_____

_____

_____

_____

(Verses to consider: Matt. 5:28; Gal. 3:10, 13; Eph. 2:1–3; 4:14; 1 Pet. 1:14)

3) Some say that we should live and let live, that it is arrogant and even wrong to question the sincere beliefs of others. What does this passage say in response to such a charge?

_____

_____

_____

_____

(Verses to consider: 1 Cor. 11:19; 2 Thess. 3:14–15; Titus 3:9–11)

GOING DEEPER

We find another warning of the dangers of false teachers in Jude. Read Jude 1–25.

1 *Jude, a bondservant of Jesus Christ, and brother of James, to those who are called, sanctified by God the Father, and preserved in Jesus Christ:*

2 *Mercy, peace, and love be multiplied to you.*

3 *Beloved, while I was very diligent to write to you concerning our common salvation, I found it necessary to write to you exhorting you to contend earnestly for the faith which was once for all delivered to the saints.*

4 *For certain men have crept in unnoticed, who long ago were marked out for this condemnation, ungodly men, who turn the grace of our God into lewdness and deny the only Lord God and our Lord Jesus Christ.*

5 *But I want to remind you, though you once knew this, that the Lord, having saved the people out of the land of Egypt, afterward destroyed those who did not believe.*

6 *And the angels who did not keep their proper domain, but left their own abode, He has reserved in everlasting chains under darkness for the judgment of the great day;*

7 as Sodom and Gomorrah, and the cities around them in a similar manner to these, having given themselves over to sexual immorality and gone after strange flesh, are set forth as an example, suffering the vengeance of eternal fire.

8 Likewise also these dreamers defile the flesh, reject authority, and speak evil of dignitaries.

9 Yet Michael the archangel, in contending with the devil, when he disputed about the body of Moses, dared not bring against him a reviling accusation, but said, "The Lord rebuke you!"

10 But these speak evil of whatever they do not know; and whatever they know naturally, like brute beasts, in these things they corrupt themselves.

11 Woe to them! For they have gone in the way of Cain, have run greedily in the error of Balaam for profit, and perished in the rebellion of Korah.

12 These are spots in your love feasts, while they feast with you without fear, serving only themselves. They are clouds without water, carried about by the winds; late autumn trees without fruit, twice dead, pulled up by the roots;

13 raging waves of the sea, foaming up their own shame; wandering stars for whom is reserved the blackness of darkness forever.

14 Now Enoch, the seventh from Adam, prophesied about these men also, saying, "Behold, the Lord comes with ten thousands of His saints,

15 to execute judgment on all, to convict all who are ungodly among them of all their ungodly deeds which they have committed in an ungodly way, and of all the harsh things which ungodly sinners have spoken against Him."

16 These are grumblers, complainers, walking according to their own lusts; and they mouth great swelling words, flattering people to gain advantage.

17 But you, beloved, remember the words which were spoken before by the apostles of our Lord Jesus Christ:

18 how they told you that there would be mockers in the last time who would walk according to their own ungodly lusts.

19 These are sensual persons, who cause divisions, not having the Spirit.

20 But you, beloved, building yourselves up on your most holy faith, praying in the Holy Spirit,

21 keep yourselves in the love of God, looking for the mercy of our Lord Jesus Christ unto eternal life.

22 And on some have compassion, making a distinction;

23 but others save with fear, pulling them out of the fire, hating even the garment defiled by the flesh.

24 *Now to Him who is able to keep you from stumbling, and to present you*
   faultless before the presence of His glory with exceeding joy,

25 *To God our Savior, who alone is wise, be glory and majesty, dominion and*
   power, both now and forever. Amen.

EXPLORING THE MEANING

4) Compare this with the exhortations of Peter. What do both of these passages say about God's judgment of those who willfully lead others astray?

_____

_____

_____

_____

_____

_____

5) What do you learn from the Old Testament examples that are cited in Jude?

_____

_____

_____

_____

_____

_____

(Verses to consider: Prov. 6:16–19; Isa. 9:15; Matt. 8:12; Rev. 21:8, 27)

6) Read Matthew 23:1–36. Do Jesus' words strike you as too harsh, too lenient, or just right? Why?

_____

_____

_____

_____

_____

7) If we are to be imitators of Christ, what should be our response to false religion?

_____

_____

_____

_____

_____

8) What do these passages say about apostasy, that is, about rejecting the truth after one has claimed to believe it?

_____

_____

_____

_____

_____

(Verses to consider: 1 Cor. 10:1–12; Heb. 3:12–18; 10:26–27; 1 John 2:18–19)

TRUTH FOR TODAY

When men's eternal souls are at stake, the church cannot be passive and indifferent. Nor can it hide behind false humility that fears being judgmental or behind false love that fears offending. Christ was supremely humble, yet He never called evil anything but what it was: evil. Christ was supremely loving, yet He never withheld a warning that might save His hearers from hell. And he had nothing but intense anger for those who by their false teachings led men away from God and directly toward hell.

REFLECTING ON THE TEXT

9) Why do many Christians hesitate to confront false teaching in our culture? What makes it hard to confront?

_____

_____

_____

_____

10) List several tangible ways you can better prepare yourself to stand firm on the truth of God in the face of so many deceptive teachings.

_____

_____

_____

_____

11) Write out what you might need to say (that is, what points you might need to make) to a friend or family member who is involved in a false or heretical religious group.

_____

_____

_____

_____

_____

_____

Personal Response

Write out additional reflections, questions you may have, or a prayer.

_____

_____

_____

_____

_____

_____

_____

_____

_____

_____

Additional Notes

KNOW YOUR PROPHECY

2 Peter 3:1–18

DRAWING NEAR

As Peter ends his letter, he addresses the topic of the end times and the judgment to come. There seems to be an interest today in the end of the world and the return of Christ. Novels with these themes are at the top of the bestseller lists; motion pictures that deal with these subjects are being filmed. What lies behind this fascination with the end of the world?

_____

_____

_____

In what ways are you looking forward to Jesus' second coming? Why?

_____

_____

_____

THE CONTEXT

We've all seen cartoons of the bearded character complete with a sign announcing: "Repent! The end is near!" This caricature is nothing more than a slap in the face of those who really do anticipate the imminent end of the present order. Such a mocking attitude has existed for at least twenty centuries. Peter recognized it in his day and wrote about it to the church in Asia Minor under his care.

Peter wanted his persecuted brothers and sisters to understand that the "day of the Lord" was certain and sure. Even though the event was delayed and the false teachers were scoffing at such a doctrine, Christ would come back and conclude human history.

Second, in light of the certainty of these sobering events, Peter called for the sanctification of God's people. With the glory of God at stake, with so many souls hanging in the balance, Christians need to live pure, exemplary lives and use their time on earth telling others the way to be saved. As you study this stirring chapter, thank God that He is in control, and ask Him to stir your heart to more holy living.

KEYS TO THE TEXT

The Day of the Lord: This is a technical term pointing to the special interventions of God in human history for judgment. It ultimately refers to the future time of judgment whereby God judges the wicked on earth and ends this world system in its present form. The Old Testament prophets saw the final Day of the Lord as unequaled darkness and damnation, a day when the Lord would act in a climactic way to vindicate His name, destroy His enemies, reveal His glory, establish His kingdom, and destroy the world (Isa. 2:10–21; 13:6–22; Ezek. 13:30; Joel 1–2; Zech. 14; Thess. 1:7; 2:2). It will occur at the time of the Tribulation on earth (Rev. 6:17), and again 1,000 years later at the end of the millennial kingdom before the creation of the new heavens and new earth.

UNLEASHING THE TEXT

Read 3:1–18, noting the key words and definitions next to the passage.

2 Peter 3:1–18 (NKJV)

your pure minds (v. 1)—un-contaminated by the seductive influences of the world. Peter regarded his readers as true believers.

holy prophets (v. 2)—The Old Testament prophets serve as a contrast to the false teachers.

apostles of the Lord (v. 2)—The apostles of Christ filled the 260 chapters of the New Testament with about three hundred references to the Second Coming!

scoffers will come (v. 3)—the ridicule of the false teachers towards the teaching of the return of Christ

1 *Beloved, I now write to you this second epistle (in both of which I stir up your pure minds by way of reminder),*

2 *that you may be mindful of the words which were spoken before by the holy prophets, and of the commandment of us, the apostles of the Lord and Savior,*

3 *knowing this first: that scoffers will come in the last days, walking according to their own lusts,*

4 *and saying, "Where is the promise of His coming? For since the fathers fell asleep, all things continue as they were from the beginning of creation."*

in the last days (v. 3)—the entire time period from Christ's first coming until His second advent

the fathers (v. 4)—the Old Testament patriarchs

all things continue as they were (v. 4)—God is absent from the affairs of the world and there will be no cataclysmic judgments; this is called the theory of uniformitarianism, the idea that natural phenomena have operated in a uniform, predictable, orderly fashion since the world began.

5 For this they willfully forget: that by the word of God the heavens were of old, and the earth standing out of water and in the water,

6 by which the world that then existed perished, being flooded with water.

7 But the heavens and the earth which are now preserved by the same word, are reserved for fire until the day of judgment and perdition of ungodly men.

8 But, beloved, do not forget this one thing, that with the Lord one day is as a thousand years, and a thousand years as one day.

9 The Lord is not slack concerning His promise, as some count slackness, but is longsuffering toward us, not willing that any should perish but that all should come to repentance.

10 But the day of the Lord will come as a thief in the night, in which the heavens will pass away with a great noise, and the elements will melt with fervent heat; both the earth and the works that are in it will be burned up.

11 Therefore, since all these things will be dissolved, what manner of persons ought you to be in holy conduct and godliness,

12 looking for and hastening the coming of the day of God, because of which the heavens will be dissolved, being on fire, and the elements will melt with fervent heat?

they willfully forget (v. 5)—In their attempt to avoid facing judgment, the false teachers ignore two cataclysmic events—Creation and the Noahic Flood.

earth standing out of water and in the water (v. 5)—In the early stages of creation, God collected the upper waters into an atmospheric "canopy" and the lower waters into underground reservoirs, rivers, lakes, and seas.

the world that then existed (v. 6)—the pre-flood world order, including the aforementioned "canopy"

reserved for fire (v. 7)—The present world system has an appointment with judgment; this time the judgment will be fiery, not watery, in nature.

one day is as a thousand years (v. 8)—God understands time differently than human beings do; though Christ's coming seems a long way off, it will not be.

not slack (v. 9)—God does not loiter; nor is He late.

longsuffering toward us (v. 9)—God demonstrates perfect patience toward the elect.

not willing that any should perish (v. 9)—God is not waiting for all people to be saved; He is waiting to receive all His own.

all should come to repentance (v. 9)—"All" refers to all who are God's people who will come to Christ to make up the full number of the people of God.

the day of the Lord (v. 10)—a technical term that refers ultimately to the future time in which God will judge the wicked on earth and end this world system in its present form

as a thief in the night (v. 10)—suddenly, surprisingly, unexpectedly, and with bad consequences

the heavens will pass away . . . with fervent heat (v. 10)—the incineration/disintegration of the universe in a fiery judgment

what manner of persons ought you to be (v. 11)—In light of these eternal events, Christians should conform their lives to God's holy standards.

hastening the coming of the day (v. 12)—"Hastening" means eagerly desiring; we are not to fear the end but to hope for it.

the day of God (v. 12)—This is different from "the day of the Lord" and refers to the eternal state under which there will be "new heavens and a new earth."

13 *Nevertheless we, according to His promise, look for new heavens and a new earth in which righteousness dwells.*

without spot and blameless (v. 14)—a pure character and reputation above reproach

14 *Therefore, beloved, looking forward to these things, be diligent to be found by Him in peace, without spot and blameless;*

the longsuffering of our Lord is salvation (v. 15)—The idea here is that we should utilize this time of God's patience for evangelism.

15 *and consider that the longsuffering of our Lord is salvation—as also our beloved brother Paul, according to the wisdom given to him, has written to you,*

Paul . . . has written (v. 15)—Peter uses Paul's writings as a support for his own teachings about the end times; he describes them as "hard [not impossible] to understand" and puts them on a par with "the rest of the Scriptures."

16 *as also in all his epistles, speaking in them of these things, in which are some things hard to understand, which untaught and unstable people twist to their own destruction, as they do also the rest of the Scriptures.*

know this beforehand (v. 17)—Christians have been warned about the existence and malevolence of false teachers and thus should be on their guard.

17 *You therefore, beloved, since you know this beforehand, beware lest you also fall from your own steadfastness, being led away with the error of the wicked;*

18 *but grow in the grace and knowledge of our Lord and Savior Jesus Christ. To Him be the glory both now and forever. Amen.*

1) What clues in this passage point to the first-century Christians' belief in the imminent return of Christ?

_____

_____

_____

_____

_____

_____

_____

(Verses to consider: 1 Cor. 15:51; 1 Thess. 1:10; 2:19; 4:15–18)

2) Verses 3–9 speak about God's patience. What is the essence of Peter's argument here?

_____

_____

_____

(Verses to consider: Gal. 4:4; Heb. 6:18; 10:23, 37; Rev. 19:11)

3) What things will characterize the day of the Lord?

_____

_____

_____

_____

(Verses to consider: Isa. 66:15; Dan. 7:9–10; Mic. 1:4; Mal. 4:1; Matt. 3:11–12; 2 Thess. 1:7–10)

4) How should looking forward to Christ's return affect our lives right now (vv. 14–18)?

_____

_____

_____

_____

GOING DEEPER

The apostle Paul also encouraged his readers with the truth of a future hope. Read 1 Thessalonians 4:13–5:11.

> **4:13** *But I do not want you to be ignorant, brethren, concerning those who have fallen asleep, lest you sorrow as others who have no hope.*
>
> **14** *For if we believe that Jesus died and rose again, even so God will bring with Him those who sleep in Jesus.*
>
> **15** *For this we say to you by the word of the Lord, that we who are alive and remain until the coming of the Lord will by no means precede those who are asleep.*
>
> **16** *For the Lord Himself will descend from heaven with a shout, with the voice of an archangel, and with the trumpet of God. And the dead in Christ will rise first.*

17 *Then we who are alive and remain shall be caught up together with them in the clouds to meet the Lord in the air. And thus we shall always be with the Lord.*

18 *Therefore comfort one another with these words.*

5:1 *But concerning the times and the seasons, brethren, you have no need that I should write to you.*

2 *For you yourselves know perfectly that the day of the Lord so comes as a thief in the night.*

3 *For when they say, "Peace and safety!" then sudden destruction comes upon them, as labor pains upon a pregnant woman. And they shall not escape.*

4 *But you, brethren, are not in darkness, so that this Day should overtake you as a thief.*

5 *You are all sons of light and sons of the day. We are not of the night nor of darkness.*

6 *Therefore let us not sleep, as others do, but let us watch and be sober.*

7 *For those who sleep, sleep at night, and those who get drunk are drunk at night.*

8 *But let us who are of the day be sober, putting on the breastplate of faith and love, and as a helmet the hope of salvation.*

9 *For God did not appoint us to wrath, but to obtain salvation through our Lord Jesus Christ,*

10 *who died for us, that whether we wake or sleep, we should live together with Him.*

11 *Therefore comfort each other and edify one another, just as you also are doing.*

Exploring the Meaning

5) What more about the "day of the Lord" do you learn from Paul's teaching?

_____

_____

_____

_____

_____

6) What do Paul's inspired words mean for believers? For unbelievers?

_____

_____

_____

_____

_____

7) What do past divine judgments indicate about future judgments?

_____

_____

_____

_____

8) Peter mentions a coming age that will feature "new heavens and a new earth." What does this mean?

_____

_____

_____

_____

(Verses to consider: Isa. 65:17; 66:22; Rev. 20:1–21:1)

TRUTH FOR TODAY

The theme of Christ's second coming permeates the New Testament and is the great anticipatory reality of Christian living. The Lord's return will be as real and as historical an event as His first coming. Believers look back to the moment of saving faith in Christ, when their souls were redeemed. They look forward to the return of Christ, when their bodies will be redeemed and they will enter into the promised fullness of salvation. In that day Satan will be defeated, the curse lifted, Christ worshiped, the creation liberated and restored, sin and death conquered, and the saints glorified.

Reflecting on the Text

9) Comment on this statement: "Those who do perish and go to hell, go because they are depraved and worthy only of hell and have rejected the only remedy, Jesus Christ, not because they were created for hell and predetermined to go there. The path to damnation is the path of a non-repentant heart; it is the path of one who rejects the person and provision of Christ and holds on to sin." Do you agree or disagree? Why?

_____

_____

_____

_____

_____

10) Why do so many people reject the loving provision of God?

_____

_____

_____

_____

_____

(Verses to consider: Eph. 2:1–10)

11) In what way can you use our culture's current fascination with the end times to be a witness for Christ this week? What friends or neighbors might you engage in a conversation about the Lord?

_____

_____

_____

_____

_____

12) As you think back over the epistle of 2 Peter, what specific lessons or principles stand out most to you? Why? How can you be a "doer" of these portions of God's Word?

_____

_____

_____

_____

_____

_____

PERSONAL RESPONSE

Write out additional reflections, questions you may have, or a prayer.

_____

_____

_____

_____

_____

_____

_____

_____

_____

_____

_____

_____

_____

_____

Additional Notes

ADDITIONAL NOTES

Additional Notes

Additional Notes

ADDITIONAL NOTES

Additional Notes

ADDITIONAL NOTES

ADDITIONAL NOTES

Additional Notes

Additional Notes

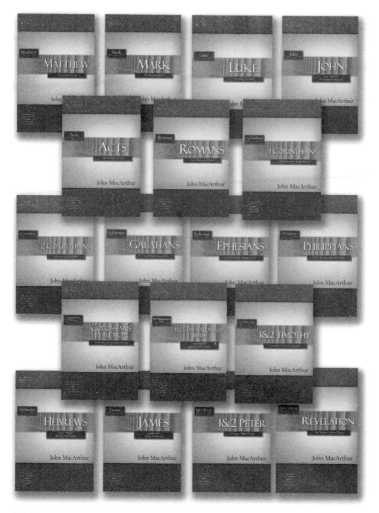

Look for these exciting titles by John MacArthur

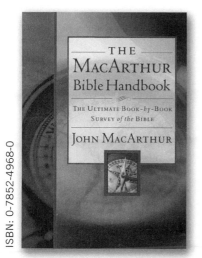